FROM DARKNESS|TO LIGHT

Teens Write about How They Triumphed Over Trouble

EDITED BY JULIE LANDSMAN
ILLUSTRATED BY RYAN KELLY

Fairview Press
Minneapolis

Published by Fairview Press, 2450 Riverside Avenue South, Minneapolis, MN 55454.

Library of Congress Cataloging-in-Publication Data

From darkness to light : teens write about how they triumphed over
    trouble / edited by Julie Landsman.
             p.   cm.
    ISBN 0-925190-36-5 : $8.95
    1. Problem youth--United States--Biography.   2. Problem
      youth--Rehabilitation--United States.   I. Landsman, Julie.
    HV1431.F76   1994
    362.7'4'092273--dc20
    [B]   94-36621
                                          CIP

First printing: November 1994

Printed in the United States of America
98 97   7 6 5 4 3

Cover design by the Nancekivell Group
Interior design by Marti Naughton

Publisher's Note: Fairview Press publishes books and other materials related to the subjects of physical health, mental health, and chemical dependency. Its publications, including *From Darkness to Light*, do not necessarily reflect the philosophy of Fairview Hospital and Healthcare Services or their treatment programs

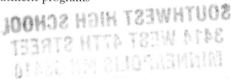

CONTENTS

7 BODY IMAGE

8 ILLNESS/DISABILITY

9 DEPRESSION

10 PREGNANCY

ACKNOWLEDGEMENTS

There is no question that this book could not have happened without the time and attention each of these young adults gave to their writing. While they are included in the table of contents, we would like to acknowledge them here and, in most cases, list their ages. Anonymous authors and authors with pseudonyms are listed with the titles of their essays.

Sara, 14
Anonymous ("The Strength to Make It")
John Masicotte, 17
Elise Clemens, 18
Anonymous ("Free"), 17
Melissa Blessing, 17
Michael Eckerman, 17
Ralph Hostutler, 14
Crystal Laurvick, 17
Anonymous ("Suicide: An Emotional Roller Coaster"), 17
Vanessa, 15
Anonymous (A Friend), 17
Courtney, 14
Constance Sheppard, 16
Christy Grover, 17
Anonymous ("My Father, My Nemesis"), 17
Anonymous ("Moving When You Are a Teen")
Jamie Cooley, 14
Cate Fogarty, 16
Denelle Wyman

Duane Whittaker, 18
Judith Welliver, 16
Andrea Anderson, 16
In Situ Angst
Kelly Godfrey, 18
Anonymous ("Making the Right Choice"), 14
Tyane, 16
Brea, 14
Tyler Shaw, 13
Alicia McMurphy, 14
Anonymous ("Obstacles Overcome"), 16
Anonymous ("Slim Chances")
Kristen Schmitz, 19
Anonymous ("Getting Started"), 14
Isaac Toso
Amber Junker, 16
Suzanne Colby, 13
Daisy, 14
Michelle Humphrey, 17
Mathew Gifford, 18
Kaitlin McLachlan, 14
Spencer Foxworth, 18
Maura

Elizabeth Neil, 17
Matthew Byrne, 17
Victoria Humphery, 14
Karla Williams, 19
Tong Thao, 18
Endu, 18
Anonymous ("My Experience during the Liberian Crisis"), 19
Khieo Souvannavong
Anonymous ("Struggle to Freedom")
Daniel Gittsovich, 14
Anonymous ("My Journey from Santiago, Chile, to Minneapolis"), 16
Dawn
Anonymous ("I Am Who I Am"), 14
Anonymous ("Not Just Half and Half"), 15
Anonymous ("Overcoming Homophobia"), 15
Kelly Hardy, 16
Jake Reyo, 16

We would like to gratefully acknowledge the following organizations for their contributions to this project. Without their help this project would not have been possible.

For their financial and in kind contributions we would like to thank:
>   Fairview Foundation
>   Minneapolis Public Libraries
>   Nemer, Fieger and Associates, Inc.
>   The Saint Paul Optimist Club
>   *Young Adult Press*

We would sincerely like to thank the following panel of judges for giving their time, talents, and hearts to the project:
>   Adela Peskorz, Minneapolis Public Library
>   Ron Mortenson, MARYS
>   Kathy Bardins, Family Times
>   Louis Henry, McDonald's
>   Bob Salisbury, Business Talents
>   Debra O'Donnell Tavalier, Hazelden
>   Reverend Marchelle Hallman, St. Paul Area Council of
>   Churches

For their individual contributions in a variety of contexts, we would like to acknowledge:
>   Tamara Crea, editor of *Young Adult Press*, for her dedication and
>   commitment to the project.
>   Amaya Olson, Paul Jung, and Alicia Olson—volunteer teens
>   who chose the winning essay.
>   Ryan Kelly, a 1994 graduate of Washburn high school, for his
>   thought-provoking illustrations. Ryan currently is attending
>   Minneapolis College of Art and Design.

We also would like to specially recognize Shannan, whose essay could have helped many other teens, but was unable to be published. Finally, thank you to Jay Johnson of Fairview Press who was such an inspiration for this book.

PREFACE

Generations of adults have been concerned about the future of teenagers. Discouraging statistics bombard us daily with grim pictures of teen violence, pregnancy, abuse, chemical dependency, and suicide.

But in our community and professional relationships, we believe that every dismal reality has its flipside. This belief caused Jay Johnson, an editor at Fairview Press, and me to plan an essay-writing contest to encourage young adults to share their success stories in the face of adversity.

We wanted the stories to reflect the authors' own resiliency and their positive approaches to personal problems. We also hoped this contest would provide healing and an opportunity to build self-esteem. The entries confirmed how it takes *honesty* to look at ourselves, but it takes *courage* to share ourselves with others. The book that is a result of this contest also shows *how* these people are overcoming obstacles in their lives.

Although many of the 500 entries were heartbreaking to read, we found them to be inspirational, and they touched us deeply. The essays showed how the authors are trying to heal and how they are helping themselves.

While this book only presents the sixty contest winners, we think they give a fair representation of common problems, worries, and approaches to difficult situations. We hope every person who entered won something during the therapeutic process of writing about their lives and courageously mailing their entries.

We hope this book will be a valuable guide for teens who are still struggling and for all adults who know and love them. Lastly, we hope that all
teens in trouble are able to find comfort, help, and—above all else—love.

Profits from the sale of *From Darkness to Light* will be donated to youth
organizations and agencies.

—*Eileen McCarthy Harness*
Community and Professional Education Coordinator
Fairview Behavioral Services

INTRODUCTION

After years of teaching young people from the inner cities, suburbs, and small towns across Minnesota, I am continually impressed with their stories and with the way they live their lives. I believe there is no more important gift we can give these courageous, often troubled, and always fascinating young men and women than to listen to them. They want to talk to us. Often they cannot show us how much they want to talk. They also want, however, a chance to be heard without judgment. I believe there is hope for real communication with young adults, if we—parents, teachers, counselors, community leaders, and friends—will simply hear them out.

This book is an excellent path into the minds and hearts of young people ages twelve to nineteen. We find here such a mixture of defiance, uncertainty, sorrow, fear, love, and anger. After reading these stories we are able to get a sense of the turbulence of adolescent years, of the seriousness with which these young people take themselves. We are struck, too, by the severity of their problems.

In a recent poll of youths, age thirteen to seventeen, conducted between May 26 and June 1, 1994, by *The New York Times* and *CBS News* , the following quotes stand out:

"While many teenagers said they would not want their parents riding herd on them, hints of longing crept through the bravado.

" 'Even when my parents are here, it's like they're not because they don't have any time,' said Aaron M., a 16-year-old who lives near Olympia, Wash. 'We never do anything. We never go out to dinner. We used to do it all the time when we were younger.' "

As a teacher, I know that the trick in understanding my students is to find the right balance between allowing them a way to explore their own ideas, values, and feelings, while exerting enough control of my classroom so that students feel safe there. I believe they need to feel deep down that someone is still in control to some degree. The following essays capture that difficult combination of bravado and longing in young people— wanting to be with adults and not wanting adults to control them. This book is enlightening to me as a parent, a teacher, an aunt, and a friend to young people in my life.

* * * * * * * *

After completing my own book, *Basic Needs, a Year with Street Kids in a Public School,* I traveled around Minnesota and other states, talking to educators, parents, and writers. All of them asked if I was going to write another book, about a new group of students. I said that I didn't think so, that it was time for young people to be telling their own stories. Thus, I couldn't have been more pleased when the publishers at Fairview Press asked me to edit this book of essays. While it is important for adults to write about what they observe and how they feel in relation to their children, students, and other young people in their lives, it is just as important that the young people themselves have a voice, a forum, a place to write or speak about how they feel and how they have met certain challenges. This book does just that: It gives adults and other young people a glimpse into the thoughts and feelings of those who have met a challenge in their lives. It is not second-hand but an immediate, first-hand accounting of events.

When I received the winning sixty essays, I was immediately struck by the honesty of these authors, by how open they are with us, their readers. They are especially open about their own self doubt, their own failings, and their uncertainties.

In reading these essays, we are forced to acknowledge that while the idea of moving to a new house or city or town may not seem like a major event to us as adults, it is agonizing to adolescents. We must also recognize how just being a teenager compounds and intensifies an already difficult life situation. In the Immigrant Experience section of the book we see how the shock of leaving home in the middle of the night, hiding out in the woods for weeks at a time, and finally arriving in the United States, is especially traumatic for someone so young. This section, especially, demonstrates how a young person's natural concerns for appearance, clothes, and fitting in, are exaggerated by the difficulty of a new, traumatic situation.

Echoing through all sections of this book is the constant perpetual need to be like others: "What do others think?" This tug between always being aware of what others will say, and wanting to be an individual, is what makes each situation especially intense for people in this age group. After reading a heartbreaking account of the death of a young woman's mother, or the effect of racism on one young man, we come away admiring their resilience and courage.

The book opens with the winning essay by Sara about living on the streets at age thirteen and, ultimately, about survival. It is an amazing story of fortitude, grit, endurance, and a sense of right and wrong. The book ends with Jake Reyo's account of being shot on the front steps of his own home as he wandered out to get a cigarette. This essay is a warning to all of us who may be complacent. I put it at the end of the book to leave us with a feeling of urgency and a need to do something before more of our youngsters are shot or killed in their own homes.

The writing in these essays varies in style and maturity, in lyricism and matter of factness. It varies in the ways our young people are varied. And this mixture of tone, style and approach gives rise to another lesson. We come away impressed with the differences in our youth: differences in race, culture, values, approaches to problems, and perceptions. We also finish this series of stories with the perception that our kids have a strong sense of yearning: a desire for direction. This book is a tribute to each author, and I hope, a signal to adults, to talk to our sons and daughters, our students, our neighbors; and especially to try to listen to them nonjudgementally, to understand their hearts.

* * * * *

Editor's note: After a separate panel of judges had selected the winning essays, I received them from Fairview Press. I then sorted them into separate groups around certain themes. Some of these essays could have fallen into two or more categories. I chose the category that seemed most logical. I then ordered the groups of essays into what seemed like a sequence that made sense. Some themes just naturally led into others.

I did not change a lot of the wording from the originals I received. I felt that the style of the writer, the tone of the essay, and the unique quality of each author's voice would come through most clearly without a lot of rewording or rephrasing. I did not want all these essays to come out sounding alike, or to be uniform. I did redo awkward phrasing, incomplete sentences, and illogical paragraphs. My goal was to make each person's story as clear as possible without changing too much of the original prose.

FAMILY PROBLEMS

t for the country's
ixed. While there
rvices to assit street
en table, her sitting,
nock, the interrogation began
me control over his future
tical behavior set in
uptured their sons
eways so much here in
when he hit me. I'd
bathroom and the kitchen table
lying in the hammock, th

FAMILY PROBLEMS

In this first section of the book we read about a variety of situations involving kids who must deal with situations such as abuse, rebellion, or unbearable fights or tension in the home. They live on the streets, escape into activities, or consider suicide.

In "Rising Up from the Underground" by Sara Jo, we could not get a more eloquent description of a young girl on the run and what it takes to survive. As she accurately says: "I have overcome my troubles and sorrow from the street." Yet she has a ways to go, and she knows it. This essay alone is reason enough for this a book.

A young woman who wishes to remain anonymous, writes in her essay entitled "The Strength To Make It" about conflicts with her mother, how a wall was built up between them and the depression that resulted.

John Massicotte opens his piece with "I have never really known my real dad." He continues by taking us on a journey to all the places, the lives he led, the abuse he suffered, and where he has come to now. He concludes with a desire to work with handicapped kids.

In order for Elise Clemens to write her story, "Good-bye Audrey" she had to talk about herself in the third person. She says of herself: "But Audrey never gave up fighting to survive." After reading her essay we feel and admire the strength she had to gather to do just that.

In her essay titled "Free" another anonymous young woman is caught between two parents with different religious backgrounds and feels restricted. She is eloquent in telling us what this meant for her and her relationship with her mother.

In a similar situation, Melissa Blessing describes why having blue hair is a "symbol to me of the struggles I've gone through in the first few years." We read what it took to get her through these years.

And finally Michael Eckerman, in a heartbreakingly honest essay, tells us what it meant to grow up with parents that made him feel ashamed and then guilty for that feeling. His is a story of the struggle to be kind, good, and do what is right.

The reader comes away from this section understanding more clearly than ever what it means when families are inconsistent, dysfunctional, abusive, or simply in difficult situations. As we see during the rest of this book, the family is essential to their happiness, and even in the best of such families, problems can arise that seem insurmountable to kids. We realize not only the importance of meaningful adults in kids' lives, but their desire to find "family" wherever they go.

RISING FROM THE UNDERGROUND

Sara

Well, last year I used to not care about anything almost, not even myself. I didn't care about my grades at all. I just know I wanted to be a dancer. I figured that was a long way from now, so why be serious about school? It's not gonna have anything to do with dancing. Right, that's what I thought.

I wasn't the only one, though. It seemed like everybody didn't give a damn what they did in school, or if they were even here. You go to people's houses and their parents didn't care either. I started being really bad. I was never home, and when I was, I was running away or fighting with my dad, listening to him call me worthless bitches and sluts. I've never had a mom. My dad has never remarried or never had a girlfriend for more than three months.

Anyway, last year I met Mom for the first time. She basically told me I have my life and she'll have hers. It's hard for me to trust any women. I don't know when they'll turn and leave.

Just before school let out, me and my dad started fist fighting. I got arrested a lot last year. Stealing, lying and deceiving all catch up with you harder than you handed them out. That's what I learned. From jail, they always sent me to St. Joe's. I always ran away. I was getting good at running away.

The last time I ran away, I convinced myself I was not coming back. My boyfriend met me on Chicago and Franklin (Avenues) and took me to his friend's house. I got used to sleeping on a different bed every night. The next morning, he had to go somewhere. He just left me standing there on a bus stop. I had an APB out for me and a warrant for my arrest. He just left me standing there. One more person who I trusted and loved (I went with him eleven months) turned his back on me.

Standing on the bus stop, I started talking to two men. They seemed nice, so I left with them. They promised me a hotel room and food and lots of money. For three weeks, I didn't call nobody. I was on errands with my new "friends." I didn't go to school. School was far from my mind. I only thought about surviving and my next meal. Money.

The hardest and easiest thing on the street is money. I never prostituted. I respected myself too much. I did keep that much respect. But, a lot of things happened to me. Men thought just because they gave me $2 for Micky D's, they should be able to have their little sex on. A lot of things happened. I'm still crying now.

I saw women prostituting themselves with their child in the other hand. I saw guys shoot at one another for $5. I saw worse. On the streets, shooting somebody for $5 is funny. Even I laughed at the time. Out of pain.

I realized I was only thirteen. I went to my grandma after a man thought I was a prostitute. I'll never forget how low I felt when he offered me 20 dollars. I thought "$20—for me—what are you doing here? Sara, go home." Then I thought, "I don't have a home." That hurt worst.

I called my grandma and explained everything. I stayed there to hide from the street. I also learned you can't be hanging with the homies on the street and doing the thang out there, and get down for what they are all about. And all of a sudden, I want to go back home and get down with school work and leave them behind. They come after you and ask you what's up. If you decide not to be down with them no more, they think you're with the po-po's (police). Then your name is out to be killed.

I thought it was funny how one minute they're your "family," and the next, your murderers.

I went to court for runaway counts, assault charges, and petty theft. I got off of probation October 26, 1993. I got back in school even though I barely passed seventh grade.

I know it seems impossible to hear of a kid going through all this. I understand. I look at some old homies I used to kick it with out there, and I find it hard to understand. Why don't they go to counseling? Counseling is just another grown up spitting the same thing your parents spit (talk about). Your teachers spit. Everybody's hollering the same thing. This summer I thought "I am sick of going home to home counselors, P.O.s and everybody else trying to tell me how to change." I decided to change with my own way.

I figured, I don't care if people think I'm worthless. I'll be able to show them one day. The street ain't gonna show you nothing but negativity. You don't realize it 'til you're out, though. I know I'm something. I know I was nothing on the street. I don't care how well my name got known to all the people on the street. I was not Sara, the girl who can, I was Sara "oh, that bitch."

I figured, I'm too good for that. I realized one day I'll be helping the very same people I was down with on the street—up to a treatment center or in court trying to prove them innocent. Naw, I can't really say all that. But I'm saying I respected myself enough to see what I can really do and who I can one day be.

I said something to myself at the beginning of this year. If I can raise my grades, not be suspended, not get in any fights, concentrate on my school work, and be proud, anybody can do anything.

I also realized that many people may feel that I'm worthless and helpless. But I can also have more than them one day, and they know it. So they try to knock me down so I can stay under them. I figured it out. You always got to try to be smarter than the one trying to knock you down.

I'm back in school. I have only missed one excused day. I got all A's and B's. I'm on the honor roll. I stay at home. I have a boyfriend that shows me positivity. He does everything the right way. And he is there for me. I do trust him.

I was knocked down once, but I came back up. Alone? Maybe, but I know many people have watched me come back up and I know I'm not alone being proud. I know that if I did what I did alone, anybody can do it. I know people need a person like me around every once in a while. Just so they know, not everything's hopeless and worthless.

I have overcome my troubles and sorrow from the street. Troubles never go away. This I've also learned, but I take care of my troubles more positively now. I don't dig myself deeper in to the underground. I'm here, and back to stay.

THE STRENGTH TO MAKE IT

Anonymous

I have conquered many problems such as sexual abuse. I have done this by not blaming myself. I've also handled years of screaming and hitting from my mother.

My story has started mainly from the screaming and hitting between my mother and me. Ever since I was a little girl I have been put down, called stupid, irritating, etc. And starting very young, a wall started building in my defense so that no one could hurt me.

Like many kids I was cute when I was young, but when I started growing my baby teeth fell out, and I started getting tall. My permanent teeth came, and they came in crooked. I had two sets, top and bottom. Everyone teased me for years about that and anything else possible.

By the time I was in fifth grade and in nine schools, I had a wall two miles thick. I was always irritable and depressed. No one accepted me. Once in a while people would try to come in and I would push them away because I was scared to death of someone hurting me, but at the same time I was crying out for anyone to help me.

During sixth grade I became friends with a person a lot like me; we were either on the phone, or doing something together. When my dad died, this friend was there for me. Then he moved when school was over. That summer came, and I got braces. Finally maybe people would accept me, and I wouldn't be so ugly and unwanted.

Seventh grade was hard for me. I didn't like myself, I had given up, and thoughts of suicide crossed my mind. So I reached out to someone. That someone helped me a great deal, but I was still empty. During the summer I really looked at myself, and started appreciating me more.

When eighth grade came, I was determined to be a better person. I concentrated on my grades, and made more friends, changed myself so people would accept me. During all this, and also accepting Jesus in my life, I've discovered that what people say shouldn't matter. You should always appreciate yourself.

I've made it rather far, but yet I'm still in the beginning. I know this and I just have to keep believing it. My wall has gone down, but my self-esteem is still rather low. I always think I'm ugly and stupid. My friends all tell me it's untrue. I disagree. It'll take time, but I've accomplished so much I know I have the strength to make it.

GROWING UP

John David Massicotte

I have never really known my real dad. I know who he is, but we don't know each other. My mom told me she only knew him for a week. I think this really had a bad affect on me. My mom was married to my stepfather for fourteen years. I fought with him and eventually caused their divorce.

At about eleven years old, I started using drugs and staying out all night. When I was about thirteen years old, I started hanging out with gangs. I did this because I wanted power and a way to get away from feelings of abandonment. My mom kicked me out, which made me feel like I didn't have a family. I lived on the streets, sometimes staying at friends' houses or even sleeping outside on park benches.

One day, while hanging with the gangs, I got arrested. I had to call my mom to come and get me. After she picked me up we went our separate ways. I called her later that day to thank her for helping me. My mom offered to let me come back home. She told me I had to go to school all the time. My mom found out later that I wasn't going. She gave me a break, but by the time I was fourteen, I got locked up for possessing a gun and pointing it at someone.

The place where I was locked up for a year was a treatment center called Woodland Hills. I went to drug classes and got treatment for alcohol. When I got out, my mom didn't care what I did. Like me, my mom is an alcoholic. It was hard being fifteen and not having any rules. I went back to drugs and the gangs.

I never went to school because I was embarrassed that I was in a Special Education class. I didn't know how to read very well. I was picked on by my friends for this. As a result, I ended up getting into a lot of fights.

I have also been diagnosed as having a bipolar disorder. This disorder makes me depressed at times and affects my moods and my temper.

When my sixteenth birthday came around, I was sexually abused by an older friend. He was about thirty years old. I was drunk and passed out when the abuse occurred. Although it felt good at the time, it didn't mean I was gay. This made me question my own sexuality. At this age, my drug use was really bad. I would go back to the guy that abused me to get drugs. I knew the abuse would happen again. It did, twice. The next time I was around him I told myself that I would kill him if he tried it again.

I was very angry at the way I was feeling and at life in general. I began to take my anger out on innocent people. I would jump them and want to fight. I didn't care how badly they were hurt. I once jumped a kid and put him in the hospital with bruised ribs and a broken nose.

Two days later I was locked up in the Hennepin County Juvenile Correction Center. I sat there for one month until I was sentenced to the Hennepin County Home School. I have to serve nine to sixteen months. I have been here now for seven and a half months. I work on my family problems with my social worker. She has helped me with my treatment. At first it was something I didn't want to do. I thought the staff was out to get me.

Things have not always gone well for me here. Once I was locked in the secure unit for getting into a conflict and hitting another resident. Now, I am working hard on going home in June. I have family counseling with my mom. We work on issues of trust, sexual abuse, and drugs. I had to tell my mom about gangs and gang fights. This was very hard for me to do.

My group here really cares for each other. They have helped me to deal with my feelings without fighting. We do something called "anger work," which helps us all deal with our feelings and get the anger out so we can move on in out treatment. I am also getting help for my bipolar disorder with medication. I am getting help to deal with my problems and feelings in the right ways.

I think I have become a better person at the Home School. I can communicate my feelings better. I have made a relationship with my mom and have tried to get to know my real dad. I have admitted to having a drug problem and I work with this. I have leaned so much.

I go to high school here. School is hard for me, but I have almost caught up and am only behind by two credits. I want to graduate from high school, and if all goes well I will graduate in two years. I value education a lot more than I used to. It is going to help me figure out what to do in life. I would like to work out in nature or with handicapped kids.

I would like to tell the younger readers that if they are facing some hard issues in their own lives like abuse, drugs, violence on the streets or whatever, don't hold it in. Violence isn't the way and your family isn't worth losing. If anyone ever wanted a friend to talk to, they could write me and I would listen.

If young people need support, go to a teacher or parent. Don't be afraid that you'll get into trouble for this. While I write this story, it makes me feel happy. You need to talk about your problems. I hope my story lets young people know that they are not alone and the only ones who have been hurt. Don't be afraid to get help.

My hard work and determination have already begun to work to my advantage. This semester I received the highest grades ever in the course of my academic career, significantly improving my grade-point average. I also applied to and was accepted at Mankato State University, where I will begin studies in the field of Child Protection this fall. I chose this field for several reasons. I have had many years of experience dealing with children who have mental, physical, or emotional problems. I can also use my own past experiences of being a foster child for nine years and interacting with social workers and social services in dealing with these children. Doing this type of work, I want to give these children the hopes and dreams they deserve. I want to help those with experiences similar to mine set and achieve their goals, and to be as successful and fortunate as I have been thus far in my life.

GOOD-BYE AUDREY

Elise Clemens

Audrey didn't understand why she had to leave. She didn't want to go. The eight years she had lived with her grandmother had been filled with wonderful memories. Grandma was everything to Audrey. One day Audrey's mother came to New York for a visit. Later that evening, after Audrey had gone to sleep, she was awakened by a loud argument near her bed. Her mother and grandmother were shouting at each other. She turned over to see what time it was—3:00 a.m. Audrey's mother ordered her to get out of bed and told her that they were leaving.

Her mother told her that she didn't have a choice of whether or not she was staying or going. Audrey started to cry and threw herself onto the floor. When she begged her mother to let her stay, Audrey's mother turned around and slapped her. She said to quit acting like a baby. All Audrey wanted was to stay with the person who loved and cared for her. She was heartbroken when she saw her grandmother's face—a river of tears. Finally, Audrey's mother said that the taxi was there and that it was time to go.

While they were in the car, her mother told Audrey that she was sending her to live with her father. Audrey had not seen him since she was a year and a half old and knew nothing about him. Not only did she have the pain of no longer being with her grandmother, she also had the fear of living with a man she had never known.

When they arrived at the airport, Audrey's mother put her on the plane and said good-bye. Several hours later, the plane landed in Minnesota. She got off the plane and was greeted by a tall man and his lady friend. Audrey figured that the man was her father. Audrey was scared, but she was determined to make the best of the situation. When they arrived home, they decided to sit and talk for a while about the new arrangement. After a couple of days, her father went back to work. Audrey figured that he must have taken off a couple of days so that he could get her settled in. Every time he left for work, his girlfriend started calling Audrey names and even hitting her. She told Audrey that they never wanted her and that she was going to ruin everything between Audrey's father and her. It was as if she enjoyed hurting Audrey.

But Audrey never gave up fighting to survive. Every time she knew that she was about to get hit, she pretended that she was in another world where no one could hurt her. Shifting her concentration lessened the reality of the pain. After a while, her father started to realize what was happening when he wasn't around. Audrey and her father decided to move out.

A few weeks later, however, Audrey's father started to regret moving out. He seemed to want to get back together with his girlfriend. He blamed Audrey and started showing anger towards her. He started to drink and use drugs. When he drank, he got very violent. One day, he told Audrey that she was no good and that she would never amount to anything.

Finally, after three years of putting up with his physical and verbal abuse, Audrey did the most difficult thing in her young life; she turned him in. When Audrey was taken out of those surroundings, she decided that she would never let anyone hurt her like that again. She was going to prove to herself that she could make it.

Now, even when she feels like she has achieved a goal, she continues to set new goals and is determined to meet them. Audrey lives with a wonderful family that has given her their last name. They have given her the positive energy she needs to keep going. They have also have given her the loving and caring environment that she never had. She will never give up, and she will succeed if it's the final thing she does in life.

I know that I will succeed. This story about Elise Audrey Langner is about me, Elise Clemens. This determination is what I will put forward to succeed in college. This is what I know will get me there, and with this I will give everything I have. I have the power to do it, and now I'm going to take advantage of it and show everyone that I can be successful.

FREE

Anonymous

jerked open my locker, and a piece of folded paper fell out—an event that ultimately led to a complete turn-around in my life. I opened the oddly pleated note and found that it was from a boy who wanted to get to know me but couldn't come straight out and talk to me. He wanted me to write him back. I slammed the locker door and rushed to Biology, eager to tell my friend Rachel about this new guy. My mind was filled with curiosity, but I did nothing in response to his note. Mom said I wasn't supposed to have anything to do with boys.

Mom and I were best friends. Sure, I had friends my age, but I was always happiest when I was with her, doing our mother/daughter things. She felt the same about me; she loved me more than she loved dad—a concept I always found difficult to comprehend. As I grew older, I began to want to spend more time with people my age. I always felt guilty when I had fun with my friends, though. I knew mom didn't approve. In this, my sophomore year of high school, it got to the point where I started to rebel. Dad didn't care what I did, just as long as it was legal and he knew who I was with. But my mom was different. Every time I walked out the door, a horrible shadow of guilt fell over me and followed me until I returned home to her protection.

"Bad associations spoil useful habits, Martha—remember that," she would say as I left the house.

I felt guilty that I had friends—that I had fun. I was finally starting to open up and get to know more kids at school. Mom did not want me to have any friends except the members of our congregation because we were supposed to be separate from the rest of the world. Dad is Lutheran, and he would never let us associate with kids from "her church." So if I tried to please mom, dad would be angry. But if I tried to please dad, mom would lay the guilt trip on me. I had nowhere to go—there was no solution. I began to hate the way she treated me. I felt suffocated. I let the anger build up inside me. I turned down many invitations to go out and have fun because I knew she wouldn't approve.

Mom did not mean to treat me that way; she was only trying to raise me according to our religion. Because of this religion, I could not have friends outside of my faith. People of this belief don't do many things that the rest of the world does. They don't celebrate holidays or birthdays. They follow the Ten Commandments strictly and anyone who sins against these laws may not be spoken to by other members of the congregation until they repent their sins.

I grew up believing these concepts because mom always said they were right. I never really thought much about if I believed in them until I examined my beliefs after I got to know Jason.

I wasn't planning on ever talking to him, but he was so persistent. He wrote me notes every day, asking me to write back or give him a call. I ignored his efforts until I had no choice but to talk to him. He finally mustered up the courage one night to call me.

"Hello?"

"Is Martha there?" he said in an overly nonchalant tone.

My hands broke out in a sweat as I realized that this unfamiliar voice could only be Jason's.

"This is," I gulped.

After a week of receiving notes from a boy I was scared to talk to, I finally had to face the fact: He was going to approach me sooner or later, and the time had come. I had to talk.

"Do you know who this is?" he asked in a voice filled with macho confidence.

"Ahh, no. Am I supposed to?" I had to form the "I don't care" attitude. I couldn't let him think I was interested.

We ended up talking for two hours. He was really funny and interesting to talk to. We talked every night and wrote notes in class every day for the next couple of weeks. I got to know him and I began to like him very much. Before, when a boy showed interest, I got scared and shied away. But Jason wouldn't let me; he made me open up and get to know myself and him. I learned about his hopes and desires and his views on life as it went on around us. He made me laugh and he made me cry. As we became closer I eventually began to tell him things that I shared only with Rachel; things that even my mom did not know about me. I really opened up to him, but not as far as telling him about my religion and the effects he was having on my practice of it. He just wouldn't understand the significance of the role it played on my life.

I was always the one who answered the phone when it rang because I did not want my mom to find out about him. She never once asked who I was talking to—she trusted that I would never go against her wishes by talking to a boy. I would also call him late at night when everyone was in bed so I wouldn't have to worry about her walking in on our conversation or picking up the phone to make a call and hearing his voice on the other end.

After a while, Jason began to constantly ask me when we could go out and do something, but I always made excuses. I really wanted to, but I just couldn't let mom down.

"The purpose of dating is to find a marriage mate," she would always say.

The people in her congregation do not date until they are old enough to marry. From the first time I was proposed to in first grade until my sopho-more year in high school, I always turned down any prospective boyfriends. But Jason was different. And I was really beginning to like him.

Our newfound friendship made me look deeper into the situation. I couldn't keep giving him dumb excuses when he asked me out and I couldn't keep talking to him every night without mom finding out sooner or later. As I got to know myself better and better, I decided that my religion was not healthy for me. I guess he was the spark that lit the fire. After living for the last couple of years with guilt and pent up anger, I finally talked to mom.

It took me a long time to figure out just what to say and how to say it. I didn't want to hurt her, but I had to be firm and not back down like I usually did. It took me three tries before I actually came out and told her how I felt. It was difficult to find the words to express my overflow of emotions. I decided to ask her to come up to my room instead of calling Jason one night.

"Mom, I want to talk to you about something," I said. "I need my freedom." I told her that I loved her very much and I respected her authority, but her rules were too restrictive for me.

"I need to live my own life and choose my own friends. You know that I have good judgment. And you've never had a true complaint about any of the friends I bring home." I cringed. "I just can't handle the guilt you lay on me anymore, and I guess what I'm saying is that I'm not going to let it bother me anymore."

"I don't understand what you are trying to tell me," was her reply.

"I don't want to be this religion anymore! Right now it is taking away all of my freedom."

I began to cry. Mom just gazed at me as if in a dream, unable to comprehend what I was saying.

"I feel trapped—I can't make any of my own decisions. I've recently realized that I depend on you for all the answers—don't you see that? I always ask you what you think of something before I do it. I always wonder if what I'm doing is right or wrong. I can't figure out anything for myself because you always have the answers for me. It's not your fault, but your answers are always religion-based. I have been thinking a lot about it lately and I have just realized that I don't always agree with your answers."

Tears streamed down her face. She looked like she had just found out that someone had died. We sat in silence, unable to look each other in the eye.

"I have felt this coming for a while," mom murmured. "We have been drifting farther and farther apart. I've felt like I don't even know you anymore . . . and now . . . I see that I don't."

I didn't know what to say. This was our last moment of closeness, and we both knew it; from now on our relationship would never be the same. Her religion is her life and now I, her best friend, had closed the door on both.

A coldness began to fill the room and still remains in our hearts. My mother gave me my freedom that night, even though she still believes there is a glimmer of hope that I will come back. I gave up all that had ever mattered to me up to this point in my life on that one winter's evening: my wonderful relationship with my mom and my religion.

But I gained two very important things: respect for myself and my decisions and freedom to make these decisions.

I still wonder when I would have been liberated if Jason hadn't come along. Would I still be best friends with my mom, or would something else have sparked to start the fire? Jason did not turn out to be the man of my dreams, but I will always thank him in my heart for the help he unknowingly gave.

Author's note: I chose not to disclose the name of my mother's religion with the intent that readers will not have ill feelings towards this group of people. "Free" was written with no intention of criticizing the people of my mother's faith, but merely with the purpose of showing the reasons for the downfall of my friendship with my mother. Although this religion was not the right one for me, it provides daily happiness for people all over the world. My mother's religion is the essence of her happiness and I am proud of her for remaining strong in her faith through life's daily troubles.

BLUE HAIR

Melissa Blessing

I have blue hair. I change it frequently to green or purple or some other bright color, but right now I have blue hair and that is part of who I am. It's a symbol to me of the struggles I've gone through in the last few years and how I've overcome the restricting boundaries of society.

I grew up in a very religious family, the oldest of six kids. I was home-schooled until sixth grade, which was my first year of public school and also the beginning of breaking away from the values and beliefs I grew up with.

My parents took me back out of school near the end of seventh grade. Because I was having problems with peer pressure and getting into some trouble, they were concerned about where I was headed. I was extremely resentful of this and fought against it desperately. I felt like they were trying to fit me into a mold I didn't belong in. I was constantly told that my beliefs were wrong and that I'd go to "hell" if I didn't share their beliefs, which were of course "the truth."

By the time I would have been in ninth grade I felt like I was trapped in a never-ending cycle, battling to prove to them and to myself that I was not a bad person for not believing as they did. By going against the values I was brought up with, I was being rebellious and therefore I had very little freedom. I couldn't get away from being told again and again how wrong I was, until I started to believe them. I lived in fear, even though I knew in my head that I was right.

As I got older it became easier for me to stand up for myself and say, "You can't tell me that what's right for you is what's right for me." But by standing up for myself I was just screwing myself over, because the more I did, the more my parents realized I couldn't be changed and therefore, the less freedom they gave me.

It got to the point where I felt I would explode if something didn't change. I was using drugs heavily to get away from the pain, because I knew I lacked the emotional strength to deal with things. One summer about two years ago I came to the conclusion that the only way my parents would ever give me the freedom I needed was if they thought I believed in what they did. So I decided to fake it. I went through a personal "revival," and it worked: gradually my parents got more lenient, but at the same time they were getting even more religious.

For my ninth-grade year, my parents decided to use a home-school program based on religion. I faked my way through it, hating myself the whole time because I wasn't being true to myself. I'd sneak out every night, and I was using drugs even more, often alone. Gradually the real me started coming through and I knew I couldn't hold everything in any longer. I told my parents everything, and then basically told them they needed to accept who I was—they couldn't take away my freedom just because I wasn't who they wanted me to be. It was one of the hardest things I've done in my life, because professing my real self meant I also had to be strong enough to stand up for who I was, no matter what.

The biggest challenge in standing up for myself, which I faced about a year ago, was coming out to my parents about being bisexual.

They, of course, told me it was wrong. I couldn't understand how anyone could think that something I considered so beautiful was perverted. There were other things: It was wrong to be "extreme in appearance" and attract attention (even if that's not the intent), and it was my fault if people looked at me and stereotyped me because of my appearance. It was endless.

My parents finally let me go back to public school in tenth grade. The conflicts between us didn't get any better though, because I was becoming more and more sure of myself. During the summer between tenth and eleventh grades, my parents decided our struggles were doing us and the rest of the family more harm than anything else, so I moved in with my grandparents.

Shortly after that I started going to drug treatment and stopped using drugs. I didn't feel the need to use them since I wasn't being emotionally bombarded anymore. I also started going to one-on-one counseling. The more I got in tune with myself, the more I realized how many of my parents' ideas and beliefs were influenced by the media, stereotypes, and our society in general. It hit me then that the struggle wasn't standing up for myself just to my parents, but to the whole world. I can't let myself be influenced by society's ideas of right and wrong.

I still see new things every day that try to subliminally affect my viewpoints, and I have to keep telling myself that how skinny I am doesn't matter, that it's OK to be attracted to both men and women, and it's OK that I speak out for what I believe. I have days when I feel that most of the continent is against me and would prefer to look at people with blue hair as criminals, not caring to see past the ignorance they've been brought up in.

So I try to just smile at the people who I know are criticizing me as soon as I walk past, and I hope that as I'm learning that it's OK to be who I am to the full extent, other people will come to that same realization—about me and about themselves.

TALL AND SHORT

Michael David Eckerman

To me life is a journey that is made up of many valuable experiences. Sometimes life deals you a situation you're not fully ready to handle until later on. My life is an amazing story of adapting to a mountainous challenge that now feels like a mere speed bump. The situation I am speaking about is my parents being dwarfs, or little people, as they prefer to be called. The obvious challenges of every-day life for my parents were apparent almost everywhere.

On February 28, 1977, I was born. This day marked one of two "miracle" days that blessed my parents with two healthy, average-sized sons. The odds of both my brother and I being average size was about one in four.

As I began to grow up, I didn't sense anything different about my parents for quite a while. To me, having short parents was nothing special.

Then one day an alarm went off inside my head. "My parents are shorter than everyone else's. How come?" This particular question was answered by my parents very simply. I quickly accepted their explanation and moved on with my life.

When the fourth grade rolled around, the problem became apparent again. I began to have friends over a lot and the moment they first saw my parents, expressions of shock danced across their arched brows.

"Hi, we're Mike's parents," my mom and dad would say.

"Hi, I'm Matt," would be the reply as they checked out the rare com-modity of my parents short stature.

I'm not trying to say that I was deeply embarrassed by my parents, for that would be exaggerating the experiences. I was just anxious about my friends' reactions.

Time marched on and so did I. Near the end of the fifth grade I remember beginning my illustrious baseball career in Little League. I attended the practices and enjoyed being able to compete with kids my age in an athletic activity. I definitely decided that I was more satisfied with playing baseball rather than soccer, so I focused all my young energy into the sport.

Towards the end of one practice my mom came up over the grassy knoll at the back of the field and began to call out my name. I immediately panicked and screamed out, "Go away, I'll be there in a second." This was just an instant reaction to a situation that I dreaded having to go through at that particular time and place.

With baseball practices came baseball games. My loving parents would attend the games and receive the usual array of glances and double takes from other parents, coupled with the common snicker or remark from young children or teens. I always wondered at the time how much these sometimes cruel remarks and obvious stares affected my parents. During my two-inning playing time I was more worried about a fly ball actually reaching me in right field than my parents being uncomfortable.

As always time went on. My eighth-grade year brought about many fun experiences for me. One was an appearance on the television talk show "Good Company." That experience was a nerve-wracking one indeed. The thought of everyone in the metro area seeing me with my short parents made my adolescent stomach turn. What would everybody think? What would they say about me behind my back? These were just a few of the questions that raced around in my head leading up to the fateful afternoon taping.

When my family and I walked out onto the stage, a rush of anxiety flooded my thoughts. I prayed that I looked all right and that neither my parents or I would say something embarrassing. The appearance was short and sweet. The nervousness wore off towards the end and I even was able to tell the audience my personal feelings regarding the topic.

That also was the last year I attended Assumption Catholic School. I dreaded having to leave the comforting walls of Assumption. Having to go to a new high school was a thought that nagged at me all summer long.

I guess it was about Labor Day when I became frozen with terror. The school work was not what I feared, but the real fear was the idea of having to go to a new school full of unknown faces that was five times the size as my old school. This fear subsided rapidly as I made new friends and found my niche.

I once again was hesitant about telling everyone that my parents were short.

"Short, you mean like 5'2"!"

"No, I mean about 4'5"."

This was the basic dialogue I had with peers whenever the subject of my parents being short was introduced to the conversation. My pulse always skipped a beat when I heard the question rolling off the tongue of a new friend.

I have to admit that much of my apprehension was greatly reduced as the years went by. Most of my fellow classmates accepted it and let it fall into their subconscious. There always was the occasional inappropriate joke or mean off-the-cuff remark, but nothing significant enough to really make me depressed or self-conscious.

Nowadays my parents chaperone school dances and attend the formal functions that celebrate my academic accomplishments. To me having short parents is like eating a piece of chocolate cake: It's great no matter what size it is.

DEATH AND DYING

t for the country's
pixed. While there
rvices to assist street
en table, her sitting,
ock, the interrogation began
me control over his future
tional behavior set in
ptured their arms I
ways so much here in
when he hit me. I'd
behind and he would hit table
lying in the hammock, th

DEATH AND DYING

The death of loved ones, from a friend on the basketball court to a young sister, affects us all. In these essays we read about how death from injury, suicide, and illness affects the young people directly involved with it, close to it. Ralph Hostutler writes about the death of his sister; Crystal Laurvick about the death of her mother; Vanessa about the death of her grandmother. The death of these family members leave the writers with feelings of guilt and sorrow and, in some cases, with a new belief in religion.

In an essay titled "Suicide: An Emotional Roller Coaster," an anonymous young man describes in detail how he felt upon the death of his friend, Jason. He describes the despair a young person feels when he loses a friend. And finally in an essay titled "A Friend," an anonymous young woman eloquently describes meeting a man at the basketball court, how she became friends with him, and how she experienced his subsequent illness and death.

In these essays we are impressed by the honesty of each of these young people and by the way they do the hard work of soul searching, trying to find meaning in these deaths that seem so unfair to them. We are taken on their journey in this section of the book. This is a journey we are all to take—the exploration of our reaction to death. These young people are excellent and compassionate guides.

THE LOSS OF MY SISTER

Ralph Hostatler

When I was only nine years old I was walking home from Tom Thumb (grocery). While I crossed the street, my sister followed with her friend. Her friend didn't get touched—but my sister got plowed over by a Ford pickup. The people in the truck kept on going, without stepping on the brakes for about four blocks. Her shoes flew about twenty-five feet in the air. I ran home! I had a cheap piece of gum, and I almost gagged. I probably ran the fastest I could, but it felt as if I was in slow-motion. I went inside my house and yelled, "Jenny got hit!" Everyone came running—I was way behind.

It seemed hours until the paramedics came, but it was only like five minutes. They gave her shock treatment, but she could not be revived. Her friend and I waited in the car and said, "We don't care if she gets paralyzed—as long as she lives." My parents came and told me she died.

I cried for days afterward. People kept coming to my house asking me questions. I couldn't take it. I just stayed in my room.

I went to the wake a couple days afterward. I couldn't even get close to her. I think I was a little scared, or maybe I just didn't believe it was her. They made me sit in the front row. I was in tears, and everyone was looking at me. People who never really knew my sister were in tears. I didn't get why they were there—they were never around when she was alive. When I looked around the wake, there were flowers everywhere—the most I've ever seen in my whole life. The kids from the neighborhood all brought her flowers. There must have been hundreds of people there. That whole night I cried; I couldn't believe it.

The next day, before we went to the funeral my parents were going through her stuff. They found two poems that she had written the night before because she was worrying about my mom. My parents did their own thing when she was alive. They were never there for her. At the funeral they read the two poems. Later the poems were published in a book. Here are the poems:

Make it right Lord
I say at night, even though I've sinned—
Make it right Lord . . .
For my blessings pray
Make it right Lord
for today is a whole new DAY!

Sometimes when I talk to the stars.
Thinking how we're so alike.
There is only one of us in the world,
although there are so many alike,
sometimes when I talk to the stars,
I think how we shine so bright,
How unique we are . . .
OH how I think when I talk to the stars.

In school she was popular and always had friends over. The teacher that she always hated and called "fish face," sent us a very nice card with a large sum of money in it.

My parents wanted me to go to counseling afterward, but I didn't. Then the summer vacation was over. That year I dealt with my problems the wrong way—I just didn't care. I would do anything. I took it out on other students. I don't even think I finished a whole day of school that year without fighting someone or getting in trouble. And this continued for a couple of years.

Now I go to the cemetery, often putting flowers on her grave. I still cry and I talk to her—I hope she hears me. I'm fourteen years old. Sometimes at night I think about it and cry. I'm finally getting over it. It's been five years now—it still hurts, sometimes really bad.

Personally, I think her friend had something to do with it because my back was turned when it happened so I didn't see it. My sister was always cautious about cars. I've never talked to her friend after it happened. We used to be close. But now she's in her own world. She used to be a straight-A student, and ever since, she has been getting in trouble. She even smashed her dad's van.

I'm going on with my life. I go to the eighth grade at Bravo! I'm doing well in school. Sometimes people ask me questions about it. It's hard to talk about it without getting a tear in my eye. I still wonder how it would have been different, with a seventeen-year-old in my house. We probably would have the same friends. I still see her old friends once in awhile. Some are graduating, some have dropped out, and some just like to party. I wonder what my sister would be doing.

I think this has made me a stronger and better person, but I wish it would have never happened. She was the best friend I ever had. I take care of her grave. I don't know why most of the other people don't, but sometimes one of her old friends will surprise me and leave stuff there.

I think I am doing pretty well with her death now. I think of her a lot. I still see her old friends. I have flashbacks when I drive by where she was hit. And yet, I think I am making it okay now. I let myself remember her and that is good.

MOTHER

Crystal Laurvick

"Good morning," I'd say as I stepped further into her sewing room. She'd stop whatever it was she had been working many hours on, walk over, then give me a warm, motherly hug. Those hugs were filled with so much love, you could feel it emanate throughout your body. I never liked letting her go back to work, but I knew I had to.

The late evening of that day came quickly and I retired for the night, like any other. A knock at my door woke me. Mom wanted to be taken to the emergency room. She had been troubled with abdominal pains throughout the night. I became concerned and had to go with her and Donna. As always, the emergency room was a busy place, but they do take the more serious cases first; I knew it shouldn't take too long before she would be seen. Dr. Joesting, the physician on call that night, saw her rather quickly. He found her diagnosis to be a hernia in her lower bowel. The sound of that alone caused me to cringe with pain. He assured us that she'd be able to return home the next morning after the surgery. Knowing that Mom would be back to normal in no time lifted a great worry from my shoulders. Donna and I returned home after our good-byes; once there, I found it quite difficult to fall back into any kind of sleep.

The sun rose, showing the sign of morning the next day. We'd be picking Mom up from the hospital soon. We arrived at the hospital in midafternoon and found Mom to be on the eighth floor. One of the nurses brought us to a room, labeled 8826. The room, pitch black, had the curtains drawn shut, blocking out any light. There lay a person in a bed covered with blankets, motionless. Disbelief shot throughout my body.

We must have the wrong room; this couldn't be my mother. Tears began to form in the corner of my eyes which became red and tired the more the tears rolled out from them. I saw so many tubes entering and leaving her limp body, machines of all sizes beeping at different intervals. The two of us stood over her with perplexed expressions upon our faces. We both had many questions that lacked any explanations. Her nurse of arrived into the room shortly to give an injection of something, I assumed it was for pain. We insisted that a doctor explain what had happened. Why was she knocked out with drugs, lying in a hospital bed?

Dr. Rousey, who had been assigned as her physician, entered the room. In his arms were stacks of papers and charts that had not yet been filed. He began to enlighten us about the situation we were faced with. A cancerous tumor had been found during her surgery. Dr. Joesting removed the tumor, along with others that he discovered upon opening up her incision further. Our faces dropped to the floor. Why hadn't we known she had cancer? Better yet, why hadn't she? I didn't understand why this was happening. My mom didn't deserve to get cancer; she's never done anything to anybody. Why couldn't this have happened to someone else?

Taking a while to calm my frustrations, I left the room and called my grandparents with the news. They didn't waste any time and were at the hospital shortly. Dr. Rousey told them what we had been told earlier. Not sure of what to do, we waited patiently by her side, grasping her cold, limp hands. Days went by and she still lay there, with no knowledge of what was happening to her. I was fearful as to how things would be after she recovered from the surgery. We had no signs of anything, yet.

As before, havoc rose once Mom finally woke up from her everlasting state of sleep. I had never seen a woman so strong, cry out in fear as I had seen my mother that day.

Almost two weeks passed, and her progress showed enough improvement that Dr. Rousey released her to our care. For all of us, any sign of progress put a little more hope back into our troubled hearts. Mom went to see Dr. Rousey the next week to follow up on her progression. All seemed to be going well. She was to start an intravenous chemotherapy treatment to keep any tumors from returning. The rest of the family and I didn't know how mom was really doing mentally. She has always been good at disguising her troubles and making life seem like peaches and cream, but looking into her pale blue eyes I could see a darkness that had never been there before.

Months passed by, but it felt like only a few weeks to us. Mom grew weaker in body with each week that passed, but she grew stronger in mind and spirit. A great change took over the mom that I knew so well. She was once a passive soul, and now she took charge making sure that whatever could be done was being done to improve her situation, no matter what the cost. Unfortunately, we all knew that the only thing left between life and death was her fight

Even though none of the chemotherapy treatments that they used worked effectively on the cancer, Mom refused to give up hope. The treatments only ran her down even more than she already was. Her body grew frail. I could begin to see her bone structure in her face and hands. Clothes that she used to wear didn't fit her body any longer and had to be given to the Goodwill. I hated giving away her belongings, as though she was gone from our lives.

I would picture Mom at her sewing table, working away. I'd then glance at her, and I wouldn't know who I was looking at. That wasn't my mother; she was not confined to the house in a hospital bed waiting for someone to bring her a glass of ice water. She was outside working at putting the new plants into the garden for this summer's harvesting. I began to get to the point where I couldn't handle being around her. I was too scared to look at her. I didn't want to have to handle what I knew was approaching.

My alarm, which I was positive that I had set, didn't go off the morning of March 9, 1993. I jumped out of bed getting ready for school, even though I was already late. I stopped in mid-stride and wandered into my mother's room. While she lay there watching "The Price Is Right," I walked up and sat beside her on the bed. Though she was dozing in and out, I knew that she could hear every word that I was saying. Her situation had gotten to the point where I had been given the task of choosing where I wanted to live during her illness. I had put the decision aside for the longest time. I didn't want to have to decide—I wanted to stay with Mom in our house. I felt at that time that I couldn't let Mom suffer any longer by not telling her what I wanted. She verbally didn't say anything in response, but I knew that she, as well as myself, felt better after I told her what I had chosen.

A few minutes after leaving the room, I was called back up there. Mom had gone into a coma; she lay there unconscious, jerking her body all over the bed from the lack of oxygen to her lungs. Before I knew what had happened, there was no turning back. She was gone. I could never have her back in my life.

Since her death, my life has been moved in every possible direction. I had to leave my house, with my stepfather in it, and move into an apartment with my mom's youngest brother. Old rules were changed and new ones were added to those I had to follow. I also had more responsibilities given to me. I could no longer be a total carefree teenager like all my friends. I had bills to pay, groceries to buy and laundry to do.

And yet, the emptiness that was inside of me after her death has slowly gone away. It has taken me a long time to realize that she is always with me whenever I need her. The hardest part, losing her, is over. All I can do now is look back at the memories I have of her and be thankful I was able to spend as much of my life with her as I did.

SUICIDE: AN EMOTIONAL ROLLER COASTER

Anonymous

People who have never suffered a major loss in their life tend to see other people's grief in black and white. For those who have suffered a great loss, the reality is much bolder than black and white. The emotional roller coaster one goes through is a different color all in itself.

I remember every detail of the day I found out Jason committed suicide. I had gotten into a minor car accident on the way to school. When I got to school, people who knew I was close to Jason kept giving me hugs and telling me how sorry they were. I thought they were talking about my car accident, so I kept saying it was no big deal.

I saw one of my friends who grew up with Jason and me, crying. I asked her what was wrong, and she got this confused look on her face. She pulled me aside and asked me if I had heard about Jason. At first when she told me, I laughed. I said to her, "No seriously, what's really wrong?" She started crying again and told me it was true. Jason had killed himself the night before by poisoning himself by inhaling carbon monoxide from his car. My first reaction was to think that this was a mistake. Why would Jason commit suicide? He had so much going for him! He was going to graduate from high school in two months. I asked Sarah if maybe it was an accident, that maybe he didn't know there was carbon monoxide in his car; but Sarah said he had left a note. I still would not believe it.

I went to first hour, and when my teacher told me, I told her it wasn't true. She looked at me funny, and I burst out into tears. My teacher immediately took me to the counselor's office, but I didn't want to talk about it. As far as I was concerned, I had hit my head during the accident, was knocked unconscious, and this was a bad dream. I went out into the hall, and started helping other people with their grief. I ended up going home at 10:00 a.m. with some of Jason's other good friends. We all kind of blew it off and acted like it didn't happen. We were all hitting our first stage of denial and it was a color of gray all in itself.

That afternoon there was a grieving session held at Jason's church. The minute I walked in the church and realized that no longer was I there with Jason, but that I was there to remember Jason, I burst out into tears. They had counselors there, but no one wanted to talk. They then had a prayer service for Jason, and I started an uncontrollable sobbing fit. I left the church to go home, and on the way home the song "Fire and Rain" by James Taylor came on the radio. Jason had introduced me to James Taylor, and when I heard the lyrics, I started crying again. I got home and ran to my dad. I wanted to turn back time. I started bargaining with God. I wanted to know if I could do something to bring him back, to turn back time and talk to Jason.

My dad told me that Jason was gone and it was going to be okay. I got really mad and started crying. I told him it wasn't going to be okay. How could it be? Jason was gone, and I didn't understand why. I calmed down a little bit and decided to go to my boyfriend's baseball game. Everything seemed okay for the rest of the night. I was calm and convinced that it was all a nightmare. I would wake up the next morning and Jason would be in school standing next to his locker where I saw him every day.

When I woke up the next morning, I felt refreshed, and was still convinced it was a dream. When I got to school though, I realized it was a reality. I saw everyone with their friends, laughing and talking. I was so angry and so disgusted. How could they act as though nothing had happened? I was very much aware that many people did not know Jason, but someone in their school had died!

As the day dragged on, I went through an emotional uproar. I was angry that I couldn't help him. I was angry that I wasn't there to talk to him. I was angry that I had let so much time go by since I had talked to him. I ended up skipping my last three classes that Thursday afternoon, and went out with some friends.

The next day was Jason's wake. I knew right away on Friday I was going to dread the upcoming weekend. I managed to find a bunch of stuff that I said needed to be done right that minute. What I was actually doing was procrastinating to avoid the wake. On the way to the wake, "Fire and Rain" came on the radio again.

When I arrived at the wake, I avoided Jason's casket. When I finally decided to face it, I spaced out. I literally imagined Jason waking up and saying, "Just kidding guys! I really got you this time!" When I snapped out of it, I still couldn't believe it. I walked right up to the edge of the coffin and wanted to grab Jason and shake him and tell him to get up and go home. A friend realized that I was in a state of denial, and pulled me back. I could not shed a tear if I tried. One of Jason's friends asked me to write something about Jason in the remembrance book. I picked up the pen, and started to space out again. I snapped out of it, and wrote a short entry about a trip I had with him the previous summer. I left the wake still without a tear shed, and went out with my friends happy as ever.

The funeral was Saturday afternoon. I arrived at the funeral with a smile on my face determined to put that same smile on other faces. The service was beautiful, and I thought it to be a good tribute to Jason; but during the service, I felt as though I did not know Jason, and in the casket before me was a man I did not know. Once again I did not shed a tear, and when they read my passage from the book, my heart skipped a beat, and my pulse started racing.

I managed somehow to get on with my life. Not a day has gone by that I haven't thought about Jason or the empty chair he left behind. It has almost been a year now, and I've cried often since his funeral. When I hear any song by James Taylor, especially "Fire and Rain," I still cry. I've even cried for not crying at his funeral.

The emotions of grieving I still have, but by keeping a journal and writing down my feelings, I've been able to deal with Jason's death. I still wonder if I could have done something to make things different. And yet, I still keep in mind the good times I had with Jason, and I know that I was one of the lucky people who was a part of Jason's life. The loss of a loved one is not just black and white. It is a confusion of colors and none of these colors seems to have the exact right place to be.

LOST AND FOUND

Vanessa

When most people think of death, they think of the end. I think of death as a beginning. It's only an end in this world, not the next. I know that people may disagree with me. And I believe that people are entitled to their own opinions. Their opinions reflect how they feel about life, love, and death.

For me, though, religion is an answer to the mystery of life. When you think of life and all its wondrous mysteries, what do you think of? My answer is your religion. My answer to death is life.

The only person who was really close to me that died was my grandmother. It did not affect me physically, but rather emotionally. I was afraid. I was lonely and afraid. I had no one to turn to. I knew my parents would not understand. My brother and sister would not be able to comprehend my emotional state. Or could they? Were they feeling as I was— alone, afraid, lost? I would never know for sure. I couldn't be certain.

So, in desperate fear, I told no one. I told no one that I was afraid of death. I was afraid of dying, my parents dying, and my brother or sister dying, who were closer to me than my grandmother ever was. I needed more than just a shoulder to cry on or someone to lean on, but rather I needed to be carried. I could not walk alone.

The night of her funeral made an everlasting impact on me. The images I saw and felt penetrated deeply into my mind, my soul, and my heart forever. I could never forget it. Every emotion that has ever existed I felt that night. I felt fear, loneliness, despair, hatred, sadness, and depression. But as the night progressed, my sadness turned into joy. My anger to happiness. My hatred to love.

I was wrong. Someone was there to help me. And that night, He did. He wiped away my fears. He carried my burdens upon His back. I saw the darkness of death, and He showed me the light of life. I had lived in constant fear, but now I live in everlasting love. He comforted me in my hour of need. He renewed my faith in Him and in life. He lifted me from the depths of despair into the path of life.

Without Him, where would I be? I would still be lost. I was wandering away. He guided me back. The only man that could save me was our Lord Jesus Christ. And He did.

That night I cried myself to sleep. My parents had no idea what was happening. I hid my feelings. I thought no one knew, and that's how I wanted it to be. I was torn up inside. I had cried for what seemed like hours. The more I thought about it, the more it scared me. I awoke suddenly. There was a bright light outside my window. A man stood there. His foreboding impression scared me. My fear still controlled me. I could not control it. I buried my face in my pillow hoping the mysterious man would leave.

He didn't, and now I can say that I'm glad He stayed. I felt this overwhelming love and safety. It's something I can't explain. I slowly lifted my head, and as I did, my fear dissolved more and more. As my fear evaporated, I realized who it was. It was Jesus. He said nothing to me. There was no need for words. His eyes said everything. I saw the love within His eyes. I felt the life within Him. The everlasting light penetrated from within His heart, from within His soul. It was the light of heaven, the light of life.

There was something else I have never told anyone before. In his outstretched arms a human bone rested. I didn't understand it then, but I found the answer in the Bible.

"So the Lord God cast a deep sleep on the man, and while he was asleep, he took out one of his ribs and closed up its place with flesh. The Lord God then built up into a woman the rib that he had taken from the man" (Genesis 2: 21-22).

This explains what I had felt, because nine months later my mother gave birth to a baby girl at the age of forty-one. When I found out that she was pregnant, I had this undeniable feeling that it was going to be a girl. Her birth explained that mysterious bone's presence. It proved that life can come out of death.

But all my questions weren't answered. For years I searched for an answer. My mother's story brought me faith. She had never told me this before, and it came to me as a total shock. She said that when her father died, she fell into a deep state of shock and depression. My father tried to console her, but he couldn't. She told me that a few days after his funeral, she was home with me. I was only three and a half at the time. She told me that she was thinking about him. She was worried that he wasn't all right. Then suddenly she felt a hand on her shoulder. She heard her father's voice say, "It's all right, Dorothy. I'm in heaven with Jesus."

My mother's simple story helped me to realize that I needed no explanation because I knew that in my heart He saved me. For years I had searched myself and my faith for an answer, but I knew then that the answer to my questions could only be found within myself.

To this day, I still don't totally understand what happened. It's not something that you can explain, it's just something you know. It's my faith. I need no explanation. He had said nothing to me, which made it even more powerful.

This poem, titled "Footprints," is my only refuge in my search for what I felt that night. The man in this poem had troublesome times, just as I did, and that is why I see myself within this poem.

FOOTPRINTS

One night a man had a dream. He dreamed he was walking along the beach with the Lord. Across the sky flashed scenes from his life. For each scene, he noticed two sets of footprints in the sand; one belonged to him, and the other to the Lord.

When the last scene of his life flashed before him, he looked back at the footprints in the sand. He noticed that many times along the path of his life there was only one set of footprints. He also noticed that it happened at the very lowest and saddest times in his life.

This really bothered him and he questioned the Lord about it. "Lord, you said that once I decided to follow you, you'd walk with me all the way. But I have noticed that during the most troublesome times in my life, there was only one set of footprints. I don't understand why when I needed you most you would leave me."

The Lord replied, "My precious, precious child, I love you and would never leave you. During your times of trial and suffering, when you see only one set of footprints, it was then that I carried you."

In his journey, this man faces death and the end of his life. I faced my fears and my questions of faith. I, too, had questioned the Lord. He answered me through his undying love and support. It was He who carried me.

He carried my cross of sorrow. He saved me from my fears. Through Him I saw death as life. I will never forget it, and it will always remain in my heart.

A FRIEND

Anonymous

We were all brought into this world for a reason. Some people spend their lives trying to find that reason. Some people just live their lives. And some people are born stricken with a disability or a disease. They soon learn the reason they were brought into the world. That is what happened to my friend, who I will call John.

The temperature was going down so I decided to go out and play some basketball. When I arrived some people were already playing, so I joined in. There was one guy there who was a little different. I mean he was not ugly. He was very good looking. He was around twenty-five to thirty years old, African-American, and there was something about him that made me want to meet him. Not his looks, but he was talking with his mouth and his hands. I mean he could speak like you and me, but he was deaf and his language was sign language.

He came over and asked me if I ever played basketball. I said "Yes."

"How about a little twenty-one?" John, my new friend, said with a grin. "That is if you can play."

"You are on. That is if you can keep up with me." We proceeded to the far side of the court.

"Ladies first. It won't be easy."

"No need. I can handle my own, but I will have to warn you."

He whipped my behind. The score was close, but he dunked right in my face. John looked at me and smiled. He also said that I needed just a little bit more work and that he would teach me. When John showed me how to dunk he also showed me how to do sign language, which I found a lot of fun.

Every day John and I would meet at the basketball court and play ball. If we were not playing basketball we would go to his car. John played Whitney Houston's song "The Greatest Love of All." "Well how would you like to learn this song in our language?"

"Sure." Every day we would sit in the grass or on his car and he would show me every word in the song. We started out by listening to the first five words. Then he would show me in sign language how those words look, and then I would do the same. I tried to learn that song. I would sing it in the morning, in school, and even when we played basketball.

Then one day I went up to the park and John was not at the court, but I thought that he had to work. Day after day he wasn't there, but I kept on trying to learn the song. Two weeks went by and that is when I really started to worry.

It was about 8:00 p.m. I was at the basketball court singing the song in two languages. One was sign language and the other was with my own voice. When his wife, Ann, said, "John needs to talk to you."

"Where has he been? I finally know the song by heart."

"There is a problem with him, and it is not about his hearing." Then I looked at Ann, and I walked to her car.

When I arrived, the place was in darkness. No lights were on except for one in the attic. I walked up there, and there he was. He looked so different. He had no hair, and he looked like a plucked chicken. He was sick and he was a lot thinner.

"Hey shorty, come in. I want to tell you something." John said with a scratchy voice.

"So what happened? I mean what is going on?" I said with a tear in my eye.

"Shorty I've got . . . AIDS."

"Oh my God," Right then I started to cry. I ran and hugged him tight.

"Shorty, please do one thing."

"What is that?"

"Sing the song, but in our language." I started to sing the song, and when I reached the bridge, John 's eyes started to close. My heart was in pieces and I tried my hardest to finish. When I did, John died. But before he died John said, "Thank you for being my friend."

ABUSE

for the country's
ixed. While there
uices to assist street
n table, her sitting,
ock, the interrogation began
ne control over his future
~~tion~~ ~~behaviors~~ set in a
ptured
~~their~~ sons I
~~always so much late~~ in
hen he hit me. I'd
~~behind the kitchen table~~
lying in the hammock, th

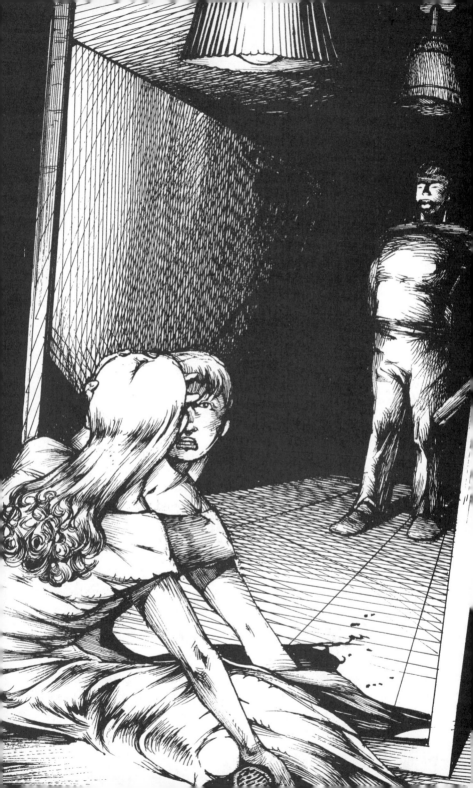

ABUSE

In this section we are inspired by the way young people who are traumatized can go on and by the fact that they can forgive. What they must be able to forgive, in the cases of these four young men and women, is being raped, being severely beaten, and being sexually harassed. These young men and women are heroes and heroines.

Courtney puts up with being called a whore, having her body handled, and having her friends desert her as she stands up for herself. At the end of the story her mother says, "Courtney, I cried at your graduation. Here, all you went through, you were still able to walk across that stage with your head held high and smile." After reading what it took her to get there, we cheer along with her mother.

Both Constance and Christy are young women who were sexually assaulted. One turns to God, the other to the advice and wisdom of her own mother. In well-written accounts of their experiences, we feel our own rage and then our admiration for their strength and their tenacity, their self-knowledge, and their willingness to be honest with us.

And finally, we are confronted with the graphic description of an anonymous young man's beating by his father. In a remarkably clear account, this author writes about how it felt to be hurt by someone he loved, ending the first section of his story with: "The last thing I remember was hitting the floor." He goes on to tell us about how his abuse was discovered and the years since the discovery.

In these essays, we have important testimony to the damage abuse can cause to a young person, and testimony to their resilience. We learn about what it takes to survive the pain of traumatic experiences.

TEARDROPS

Courtney

How many times have I cried all by my lonesome
curled up in a ball telling myself
that everything is gonna be all right?
With my tears come self-discovery,
with each discovery a nail, a piece of my innocence dies
from that cruel disease: maturity.
And with maturity comes remembrance
as anger pours over me piercing my heart.
My tears turn to those of Jenny.
I realize all I have to do is let go, let go,
just learn to let my anger and frustration
bring forth burning tears
Stormclouds burst, cooling my face
as my sadness pounds in time to my heartbeat.
I realize I am not alone, not alone, I have never been alone.

I know that as far as poetry goes "Teardrops" is nothing special. Another nonoriginal concept is that of beginning a piece of writing with a poem, but you know what? I could not care less if I tried. "Teardrops," although not written in "that time," reflects my feelings in the most difficult time in my life—eighth grade. Just an advanced warning: I'm sure some of you are going to say that I'm "overreacting" or that I'm "overly sensitive." So, don't worry, you're not alone.

My eighth grade at a school, which will remain nameless, was fairly—how can I put this delicately—traumatic. It all started on the annual beginning of the year bus trip. One of my classmates would tug on the shoulder strap of my bra and comment on the color, fabric—whatever. He did this until I told him that that was sexual harassment, and that I wouldn't tolerate it. His ever-so-brilliant response was, "I thought we were friends," to which I replied, "Friends don't treat friends like pieces of meat." I don't think he really understood, but he got bored and found other girls to man-handle. He didn't bother me again until we got back to school. Then he got the bright idea to measure my bra size with his hands. You can breathe now, he didn't get close enough. I smacked his hand away and asked to be moved. I asked a teacher for help but was met with a condescending look and placating words, and I suspect a wish that I would forget about the whole issue because, after all, this was not an "inner city school," and these types of situations did not exist in their establishment.

Needless to say I wasn't too popular for a while. When confronted with why I was causing trouble, my reply was that my mother did not raise me to let boys treat me like a slut. This got twisted into my calling other peo-ple sluts. Guess which version people believed? After a while, things calmed down, and I didn't have too much more trouble except for the occasional nickname of bitch, crack baby, slut, and my favorite, "Whore."

Like I said, things calmed down until around January. In art class we were discussing Michael Jackson. I don't know why but we were. One boy felt the need to make a comment on how alike Michael and I were. He said that we were alike because "the only condom you've ever seen is the one 'your dad used on you.'" I don't know which hurts more, the implication or that it was said about my dad. I feel the need to point out that this boy apologized for that, but his treatment of me still hurts.

THE WARNING

Constance Sheppard

My First Love. Oh, did I ever look forward to it. I wanted someone to care about me, someone to make me feel special. A lot of my friends had boyfriends, and I thought it was so grownup.

I knew it right when I saw him, I knew he was The One. Charming, intelligent, fabulously cute, and sixteen. He was three years older than me and the object of much adoration. It didn't matter that he was dating a friend of mine, because I knew. I knew that he was The One. My First.

His name was Brent. I remember the first time I met him. It was early October, and the trees that lined his street wept tears of gold, brown, and scarlet, mourning the loss of summer. The wind had picked up, and it put a skip in my step as my friend and I neared his house.

There he was, sitting on the front steps of his porch, smoking a cigarette and looking about as cool as I had ever seen a boy look. He grinned. My heart skipped a beat. Mallory, the friend that had ceased to exist in my mind until that moment, ran up and plopped down on his lap.

"So, you must be this Connie girl I've been hearing about." His voice was like honey, the words so tangible that I felt as though I could almost taste the sweetness of them. There was such a fluttering in my stomach that I had to sit down, for fear of losing my balance.

We sat outside and watched the sun set, none of us saying very much. A friend of Brent's showed up, apparently for my benefit, but I paid him no attention. I spent that night, and many others after that, watching sunsets with Brent. He and Mallory stopped seeing each other the day after we met, and Brent and I started seeing more and more of each other. After three weeks of sunsets and poetry, Brent took me deep into the wooded bird sanctuary and professed his love for me. My obsession for him consumed me like fire, and I felt not that I wanted to be with him, but that I wanted to possess him, engulf him.

His incredible jealousy amused me, and I readily dropped all male acquaintances at his request. I loved him with all my heart and desired that he be happy and satisfied at all times, if occasionally at my own expense. I sought my own identity in him. I could not love myself. But I thought that if I could love him and then make him a part of me, then possibly I could eventually learn to love myself.

One evening, he invited me over to his house for dinner. I immediately jumped up, leaving my homework scattered all over, my pencil on the floor, and started off to his house.

Walking down the newly shoveled street, I gazed around me, fascinated at the way the full moon reflected off the snow, making that early December evening seem magical and eerie. When I arrived at his house, he greeted me with a kiss, and then pulled me into the dining room, where the candlelight table had been elegantly set for two. I nearly swooned.

Without further ado, he lifted me up and sat me down on the dining room table, and began kissing me with more vigor. Being so close to him thrilled me to my very fingertips, and I shivered as his kisses seared down my neck and over my shoulder. His hands had begun to inch their way down my pants. I felt him fumbling with my zipper. Gently pushing him away, I crooned in his ear, "What's for dinner?"

"You," he replied, getting back down to business with my zipper.

"I'm serious," I said, pushing him back a second time. I was beginning to feel nervous.

"So am I." His voice was gruff as he jerked me back towards him, and started pulling at my shirt.

"Brent," I said, my voice raised slightly. "Please, stop."

"What's wrong with you all of the sudden?" he asked, and for a moment there was malice in his eyes.

"N-Nothing," I said, forcing myself to smile. "I'm just hungry, that's all.

"Why don't we have that dinner now?" My voice was trembling slightly.

"Do you really think I invited you over here to have dinner?" He had succeeded in tugging my shirt off and was now starting in on my pants again.

"Wait just a minute . . . ."

I was starting to become angry, and this time I shoved him away with all of my might. He went flying back and slammed against the wall. The fire that flashed in his eyes was like nothing that I had ever seen before. In a moment's time he was before me, and even as I heard the resounding whack, there were purple spots exploding before my eyes, and I could feel myself sinking into soft, warm blackness.

I awoke to the sensation of bombs going off all around my head, and I was having trouble opening my right eye. I was lying on a couch. When I looked up, I saw Brent sitting at the other end of the room nursing a bottle of vodka. Slowly pulling myself to my feet, I eyed him warily. He looked up.

"Did you have a nice nap, baby?" He flashed me a grin that, a week ago, would have melted my heart, but I focused on the pounding in my chest.

"I'm sorry about before," he said, lighting a cigarette. "But I hate it when girls push me."

I took a step forward, staggering slightly. "I have to leave," I said, trying to keep my voice low and calm.

"No, sweetheart, you don't need to leave yet," Brent's voice sounded higher than usual, and a little panicky. "Sit down with me for a little bit." He put an arm around me, but he seemed wobbly.

The stench from the vodka permeated my lungs, and I had to fight back the gagging sensation that had slowly crept its way up the back of my throat.

"C'mon, hon," he whispered, and motioned back towards the couch. In a sudden burst of energy, I wrenched out of his grasp, and ran, sobbing, out into the night.

As I made my way home, I allowed my mind to wander back to all of the advice, all of the warnings, all of the experiences shared with me by my mother in her desperate effort to keep me from getting hurt. I wonder how I could have lived with someone so wise and not ever have known it.

I NEVER THOUGHT IT WOULD HAPPEN

Christy Grover

The first time David and I had ever been alone together was about the worst time of my life. The two of us have known each other since we were nine and eleven years old, and I liked him as a friend. I really thought I knew him and could trust him, but for some reason on this occasion, I felt scared and didn't want to be with him.

Our two families had gone to a concert at a lake. We were supposed to be having a good time and celebrating. That was the last Friday my brother, Scott, was going to be home. The following Tuesday, he was flying down to Florida to join the Navy.

My brother, Tim, had just left David and me after playing soccer. I guess I should have gone with him. Our families were watching the concert while David and I were in an open field, with no one around.

Then, everything just happened all at once. He forced himself on me and tried to rape me. He said that he loved me, and this is what people do when they are in love. He didn't seem to care that I didn't love him, or even at this point, that I was very hurt and angry at him. I was terrified. There was nothing I could do because he wouldn't let me move. All I could say was "David, stop!" Every time I said his name, he stopped and asked what he was doing wrong. I couldn't believe he didn't know, and he scared me too much to say anything else. I was scared silent.

I don't know what I would have done or where I would be now if I didn't know God personally and stick to what I believe in. At the young age of thirteen, I couldn't take on the fifteen-year-old "bully" all by myself.

David and I were both from Christian families, and I never pictured him as being the kind of person that would hurt someone else so terribly and only care about himself. I never thought David would be so cruel to me. It shouldn't have been me that was so hurt. I wasn't afraid to speak out to my friends. Talking about it with them really encouraged me and helped me to go on with my life. Although they could not really make everything better, a friend was always willing to listen.

This happens in papers and magazines, but I never thought it would become part of my life, forever. At first, I blamed myself for what happened because we were friends, and maybe he thought I led him on to thinking I was in love with him as he was with me. Then I realized it was not my fault; it was his. Because I refused to cooperate with him, he gave up on me and left. I had to walk back to my mom as if nothing had happened, because I couldn't get up the courage to tell her what he had done to me. I was afraid she would think I was lying, to get back at her friend, David's grandmother. I did tell her a few weeks later, after he had gone back home to Denver.

I will never forget the day, Friday, August 10, 1990. Even now, years later, on the day of the incident, or when I go back to the scene, I remember and get extremely hurt and angry at him for using me like that.

I didn't see David for two years, but then he came back. I stayed away as much as possible, and he tried to act as if nothing had happened between the two of us. My mom said that it looks like I have forgiven him, but I don't know if I really have. It's hard for me to let go of the pain and forgive someone who hurt me so deeply, and I'm afraid he might try it again, only worse. I don't know how many other girls are his victims, but I do know I'm not the only one. My friend and I talk about it all the time, because he has also tried to rape her. I feel terrible for everyone that has gone through the same experience as me. No one deserves to have to go through this traumatic time.

MY FATHER, MY NEMESIS

Anonymous

The night before the abuse started my family had been out on the town and were up quite late. So when I got home I, of course, went to bed. When I awoke the following morning I was still quite tired. I dragged along and it caused me to be late, and ultimately miss the school bus. This, for some reason, sent my father into a rage. I looked into his brown eyes and saw something that I had never seen before. I could almost smell it in the room. There were a thousand fires burning at once. Sparking, popping, and shooting rage towards me.

It was quite shocking for me to see this coming from my father. From times past all I could remember was love and affection. But now, for some reason, things had changed. He yelled something which I could not decipher and I knew I would be in trouble. So I got up quickly and ran as fast as I could to my room. But he was close on my heels. I got into the room and backed myself against the bed just in time to see him burst through the door. He snarled something about me running away from him when he was going to spank me. So it turned out, I was in even deeper trouble for my reaction.

My father came toward me. He told me to bend over the bed. I refused, knowing that more than a swat on the behind was going to be coming my way. This enraged him even more, and he grabbed me by the arm and ripped me over to him. He put me on his knee and threw a few smacks down, but apparently couldn't get a good enough angle, so he stopped and made me face the bed and bent me over it. It was then I heard the belt coming off. As it slid through the loops, it would catch and he would utter, "Oh Shit."

It finally came loose. He pulled my pants down, I started to cry, and he got even more angry, and told me: "I'll give you something to cry about."

He put one end of the belt even with the other, brought it back past his waist, and, with more strength than I expected, brought it down on my bare bottom. The more I asked him to stop, the more he hit me, and the harder he hit me. This continued for quite some time until I went limp. The last thing I remember was hitting the floor.

I awoke laying on my stomach. When I went to roll over on my bottom, I wanted to scream; the pain was so great! I stood up. I realized I was in my own room. As I opened the door to leave I saw my dad standing at the end of the hall. He turned around in time to see me go into the bathroom. He came in right after me and asked me if I was ready to go to school like a big boy. I started to cry again and slowly walked out of the bathroom and went to the closet to get my coat and school bag. I slipped the coat on, picked up the bag, and walked out to the van. My dad grabbed me by the waist and lifted me up into it. I immediately ran to the back of the van and wondered what was going to happen next. He got in and drove to my school, which was only a few miles away. When he stopped, I grabbed my backpack, opened the sliding door, and stumbled into the school and to my classroom—not daring to look my father's way, not daring to say anything.

I told the teacher what my dad had told me to tell her: I had been up late the night before and my parents had allowed me to sleep in. She nodded her approval and told me to take my seat. I shivered at the thought of having to put weight on my rear end. I went to my seat and tried every possible position, but there was absolutely no way I could sit and be comfortable.

I gritted my teeth as pain soared through my rear and down past my hips, and to my kneecaps.

The next thing I knew I was walking down the hall to the nurse's office. My teacher had sent me because she must have sensed something was wrong. No. I remember as I write this now, it was more than she just sensed something. When I bumped my rear on a desk I immediately burst into tears. As I walked, I felt a throbbing in my legs. When I got to the nurse I handed her a note my teacher had written. She told me she would take a look. So I pulled down my pants, and turned to face the mirror. I heard a loud, gasp, and as I twisted around to look into the large mirror, I saw what I couldn't believe. My whole body from my bottom to knee caps were black and blue. The nurse just stood there in a daze, staring at me as though I was some sort of freak of nature. Suddenly she grabbed me by the shoulders, and turned me and made me face her. She asked me "Who did this?"

I immediately flashed back on my dad warning me of what could happen if I told anyone. He owned a gun, and a gun could kill somebody. "And I didn't want Mommy to die now, did I?"

I just said that I fell out of my bed. She shook her head, and asked me "Did Mommy or Daddy do this to you?" And at the mention of Daddy, I put my head down low and began to sob quietly. But I didn't say anything. She must have known that was a yes, because she pulled my pants up, and walked over and searched though a file cabinet full of small white cards. When she found the right one, she walked over to the telephone and dialed a number.

"May I speak with Barbara Wilson please? Thank you." A minute later she said, "Hi—Mrs. Wilson, this is the school nurse at Snail Lake Elementary. Steven seems to have become sick with something and we were wondering if you could come and get him? OK—thank you, we'll see you in a little bit."

About five minutes later, I heard the office door open, and I jumped off the bed I was laying on and ran out into the main office to see my mom and the nurse conferring. I ran to my Mom and she picked me up, not knowing what had happened earlier. I shrieked out in pain and began to cry again. She looked puzzled, and the nurse told me to go in by the bed and take my pants off so we could show what was wrong to Mommy. I did as I was told. The nurse and my Mom followed in right after me. I undid the button, and the zipper. But I hesitated when I went to pull them down.

The nurse smiled weakly, and told me, "It's OK, nobody's going to hurt you." I slowly pulled them down and revealed the horrible sight. My mom stood in shock, not wanting to believe what her eyes were telling her she was seeing. She walked over, and I could see tears start to form and run down her cheeks. She told me to pull my pants back up, and to go out and get my stuff from my classroom. I heard her say as I was walking out, "We are going to take care of this right now."

"Oh, David," I heard her say, as though speaking to my father. "What have you done? You're in trouble now."

About a year later, after one more instance of abuse, my mom told my dad she wanted a divorce. My dad didn't contest and he moved to Oregon where he presently resides. I continue to live with my mom.

This story is true and is dedicated to my mom, whose hard work and perseverance have made me the person I am today. You are the greatest.

MOVING

t for the country's
rixed. While there
ervices to assist street
en table, her sitting,
nock, the interrogation began
me control over his future
tional behaviors set in a
ptured their sons I
always so much here in
when he hit me. I'd
destair and he would hit
lying in the hammock, th

MOVING

In this section there are six essays on the same theme. Adults reading this part of the book will quickly realize that something that seems to be a regular part of life in the United States today can be traumatic for young people.

Moving was always a part of the young writer's life in the opening essay. However, each time she moved it was a difficult adjustment and it hurt more as she got older. In the essay she describes how she has come to cope with her nomadic life.

Jamie Cooley has moved four times in her thirteen years. She writes: "It is not as easy for my mother, my brother, and me to just 'pick up' and leave our town. We seem to get very attached to our surroundings, and that makes it awfully hard to leave" Yet she ends up by saying that moving has been both the best and worst of her experiences in life—a tribute to her flexibility and ability to change.

Cate Fogarty moves from her idyllic home in the Caribbean to Minnesota. She finally escapes into books after her classmates laugh at her clothes. Eventually, she finds some friends and now seems to be doing fine.

Denelle describes leaving people and places she loves to move to a small town. This was a series of moves, actually, that was painful each time. Near the end of her essay she says: "If my life was a watercolor painting, it was at this point that the colors all bled together and the image faded away."

She seems to express, in this metaphor, the way many of these young people feel when they start a new school and come to live in a new, unfamiliar environment.

Duane writes about leaving his public school to go to a private school. As he describes it, this move was made because "I was having far too much fun going to school with my friends than I needed to." Duane is African-American and when he gets to Minnehaha Academy, he finds the population mostly white. This causes him problems. He learns from this situation eventually and ends his essay on a note of satisfaction and gratitude for the challenge.

And finally, we read about Judith Welliver and her move to an Amish community. "We had to live with no electricity, no refrigeration, no running water, and no indoor plumbing for five months." In fascinating detail, this young woman goes on the describe the way her family adjusted to a way of life without much of what we take for granted. By the end of her time there, she begins to enjoy it and gives us real insight into our own lives.

These young men and women have found ways to cope with something that may seem incidental to us. To them it was a real challenge and as you will read here, each one met this challenge head on.

MOVING WHEN YOU ARE A TEEN

Anonymous

It was a warm and sunny day in June when my parents made their final decision about our move. I had just gotten out of the sixth grade and was looking forward to going into junior high in the fall with all my friends. My parents, however, had decided to relocate our family to Minnesota during the summer because my mother had been given an opportunity for a promotion to work in Saint Paul as a manager of a mortgage company for First Banks.

My family had moved several times before from Billings, Montana, where I was born, to Texas; from Texas to Colorado, and from Colorado back to Montana where we started because of where my parents' jobs took them. Every time we moved it was like starting over again because I had to make new friends at each place we lived. For me, this started when I was two and a half years old. Even though I had to make new friends whenever we moved, it didn't get any easier for me as I grew up because I became very shy. When we returned to Billings, it seemed like we were finally going to stay in one place. I had made some of my best friends in grade school during the last four-year period that I lived in Montana. I lived in a rather small city so I was able to see my friends a lot because they were not more than two blocks away from my house. It was hard to say good-bye to them. After all, I would have to go to a state and town I had never been to and then was expected to settle down and make friends.

Making friends when you are a teen is not as easy as it was when I moved to Colorado in first grade, or back to Montana in third grade. Making friends was a lot simpler then. Being in the same classroom every day with the same children and playing at recess together made forming friendships come naturally. Changing classrooms with various different groups of students makes it difficult to develop friendships with other classmates and being shy complicates things even more. When you are going into junior high or high school, have just moved to a different place and you don't know anybody, it's hard making friends because most cliques have formed by then. It's hard being the outsider. The thing to do is take a chance, speak out, ask a question of a fellow student—one that you would like to get to know better—about homework or about an after-school activity or something.

It's been almost two years since I moved to Roseville, Minnesota, and I have made many friends here and I am making more every day. I took the first step when I went to a seventh-grade school dance at the beginning of the school year. I started to talk to someone, and then she introduced me to some of her friends. By the end of the first year I had made a lot of close friends.

Another way to make friends is to become involved in after-school activities. I made friends by getting involved in dance and music, two of my favorite activities. I joined the school Chamber Orchestra as a first violinist and auditioned to be in the orchestra for a school play. I have taken Ballet, Tap, and Jazz lessons since I was four years old and continue that discipline at a Roseville-area dance studio twice a week. I am also involved in the school newspaper that allows me to get to know the students and teachers better. It gives me an opportunity to learn more about other extra-curricular activities at my school. In addition, I volunteer as a preschool teacher's assistant on Sundays at my church. By doing this, I not only make a contribution to my church community but it has enabled me to become familiar with the other volunteers at my church who also go to my school.

I guess I'm fortunate that I enjoy juggling a somewhat hectic schedule of school and extra curricular activities. It has helped me to overcome my shy nature and allowed me to become involved with my school, church, and civic communities. These activities have made me a more outgoing person. Even with all these other interests, I have managed to maintain a position on the "A" Honor Roll.

When I first arrived in Minnesota I wasn't sure that I would be able to make so many new friends. I also didn't know that Roseville had so much to offer to my age group. My first impression of my school was somewhat frightening because it was so big.

When I look back on my first year here in Minnesota, I realize how many friends I have made and that things here aren't as big and overwhelming as they first appeared. It just goes to show you that you can do anything if you put your mind to it.

I'VE GOT TO KEEP ON MOVING

Jamie Cooley

Though many don't realize it, thousands of people move from city to city every year. To some, the move is the best thing that has ever happened in their lives. To others, moving has ruined everything that they have worked for and loved.

I have moved four times in my thirteen years, so I know about moving—how it can help—but, especially how it can hurt. My family and I have to move for my dad's job. He can't get a promotion if we don't move. With a promotion comes more money, which we can always use. In other words, I'm making my first point of how moving can be good for my family. If we move, we get more money.

My dad is comfortable with moving, considering his father was in the Army. Dad has lived in eight states of the U.S. and even lived in Germany. It is not as easy for my mother, my brother, and me to just "pick up" and leave our town. We seem to get very attached to our surroundings and that makes it awfully hard to leave.

I will say that the very hardest thing about moving is leaving friends. I have lived in Minnesota for two years now and still miss friends from past moves. Sometimes after saying good-bye to friends, that strained feeling in your heart never goes away. As I sit here writing this, I feel the yearning for the companionship of those that I have known for years—my friends across the Midwest. It's sad that some people don't keep in touch with those friends that they don't see very often. Through the years I have known many different people that I have written back-and-forth to in the past. Because it's so hard to write to so many people, I now only have one person I write to. I miss hearing from the others, but people change. They change . . . I change. It is funny sometimes how humans think. I always think that if I were to return to the city I moved from, that everything would be exactly the same—that I would fit in the way I did before.

My dad often has to remind me . . . people change. One thought that kept me from feeling so bad during my move is the famous saying of "Make new friends, keep the old. One is silver, and the other gold." This saying is absolutely true and reminds me that it is okay to have new friends because it doesn't mean that the others don't mean anything to me.

I've talked to so many kids who have moved or have had friends that have moved. These people are very special because they can handle one of the toughest situations that anyone could ever face.

There are two words that people across the world use several times a day. These two words are good-bye. When I say good-bye, I sometimes think of those many times that I have had to say good-bye in the past and hope that I will never have to say these words with a sad thought again.

But now enough about these sad stories, many good things also happened to me because of moving. I will explain to you some of the ways that I tackled these situations and made moving a positive experience for me.

I am very outgoing and love people and being around people. I like to be the center of attention and be involved in whatever is going on around me. If I had never moved, I have no idea what I would have turned out like. I could have been a quiet, self-contained person. Both of these types of people are great, but I'm happy to be who I am. Being outgoing makes it really easy for me to make friends and quickly find a way to fit in when we move. I usually just jump right on into my new life in this new city. For me this personality is perfect for the kind of life I have.

As I said before, I love being around people, so moving to different areas are a great way to meet different kinds of people. Most of the places I move, the people talk in a different dialect. Down in Ohio some people had a kind of southern tip on the way they talk, while here in Minnesota—well I still haven't completely figured out the way they talk! My friends and I sometimes joke about how we talk different, but I love hearing the different ways of speaking.

The one thing that has impressed me the most about Minnesota is the weather!! Right now it is April 29 and we have at least two inches of snow from a surprise storm. Last week at this time it was at least seventy degrees! Now it's snowing. It's unbelievable!

To wrap this up, I will tell you all that moving has probably been both the best and the worst thing that has ever happened to me. So if any of you are expecting to move, you may keep these things in mind. They may make your move easier for you.

ANOTHER FACE IN THE CROWD

Cate Fogarty

My story is actually quite plain—just another typical teenage-fitting-in tale. But that's what being a teenager is all about, right? It's the one time in your life when you can't escape being corny. Everything you feel can be classified and stereotyped as something everyone goes through. We are trapped in a maudlin disposition that, while we can't escape it, we seem to enjoy it in a sadistic way. So even though everything I am going to put down on this paper has been said a thousand times before, it does not lessen any bit of the experience for me or anyone else who has or will go through it. All teenagers ask for is a little understanding. We know we seem trivial and stupid but it isn't because we choose to be; it's because we are teenagers.

When I was twelve I was admittedly just another mindless follower of fads and what not. I hadn't really started thinking for myself yet, so things were just dandy. Then my parents decided that they needed to leave the paltry world entrapping them in its materialistic ideals and took my younger sister and me with them. We bought a sailboat and moved to the Caribbean. There really was no adjusting period. We were merely shoved into this different climate with its foreign peoples and slower rhythms. But being only twelve and eleven we hardly blinked an eye at our new surroundings and acclimated to them as any young people surviving in a different habitat would.

For two wonderfully full, though heartbreakingly short, years we lived like vagabonds in the sea and sun. In that warm weather ideas and beliefs tend to form earlier, perhaps too early. My sister and I became mature and responsible at ages when most are still ensconced in cheap dreams of physical beauty and social popularity. We lived with people much older who helped mold us into free thinkers and gave us intellectually stimulated minds. We talked about the stars and foreign countries. We made friends faster and cherished them more. People were more real; they did not care what kind of clothes you wore or music you listened to. I was able to be my uninhibited self.

However, this paradise could not last forever. The American ideals of money materialism, which we had tried to escape in the Caribbean, finally caught up with us and we were forced back to the U.S. for financial reasons. This did not really upset us too much; we thought of it as another adventure. It would be fun to see how things had changed.

The first cold blasts of a coming Minnesota winter should have forewarned us that our optimistic outlook was more than a little rose colored. I had forgotten the pressures of fitting in; but, on my first day as a freshman at Minnetonka High School, I was painfully reminded of them.

Being the individual I was, I had my own ideas of behavior and dress. I was open-minded to others and welcomed as much diversity as they had to offer. But as my first day progressed, I realized something very quickly. Many of the people I saw not only looked the same but acted and thought the same way as their friends. Girls snickered at my clothes and boys in the hallways told me I was ugly. Not one person sincerely made an honest effort to welcome me that first day. I was alone and ostracized by everyone I met.

Four months passed by in much the same way. I had no friends, people wouldn't talk to me or offer any friendship. It was hard to feel, in cold reality, how cruel our society can be to anyone who varies from the cardboard cut-out norm. I tried not to let my loneliness bother me but that was a joke. Days without friendly hellos are hard to ignore or forget. In class I was hated because I wanted to participate in discussions. I intimidated others because I found class easy and boring. I was the class nerd. But somehow the hot weather in the Caribbean had toughened me and, even though I wanted to fit in, I never once changed any of the things that repelled the people around me. Some days I even gloried in the fact that I was an outcast; at least I was free to be myself without worrying what people thought because they didn't like me anyway! More often than not, it was very difficult and I would wind up on the floor of the girls' bathroom crying. Just one stupid, insignificant comment from someone could hurt me so badly!

It didn't matter to me that I was different, but to have no friends whatsoever was more loneliness than one person can take. I think my hatred for the way I was being treated saved me from assimilating into their mindless droves. Whatever I did, I would not become like them for them.

During that time I had to do something to keep my mind off my troubles. I ended up doing a lot of homework and reading many books. I kept myself going by believing that it could only get better and not worse. And though it took a long time I finally won my own place among the crowd. People eventually stopped gaping at my outfits or snickering at the words I chose to articulate with. And at the risk of sounding conceited, I might add that people started asking me where to get my kind of clothes and how I had learned certain words. All I had to do was outlast them!

Today, though I no longer worry or care about how I fit in, I am planning on leaving my high school, perhaps because I have never quite gotten over the resentment and hurt that they first caused me. I don't think I will ever completely lose the lonely, sad, new girl inside me. At least I like who she is.

MY SEMI-PERFECT WORLD

Dennelle Wyman

Switching schools is hard enough as it is, let alone making new friends. Having to cope with terminating old relationships and starting new ones isn't easy. I don't know for certain that I will ever make sense of what it all means, but I hope that the struggle will make me a stronger and better person in the long run.

I was eleven and a half or twelve years old. My best friend was Lora and the worst problem I could have had was mismatched clothes or a bad hair day. My days were spent idly watching television, listening to the radio and dreaming of being like Paula Abdul. Since that year, everything in my life has changed completely, in some ways for the better, in some, for the worse.

I started junior high; it was radically different from elementary school. Lora and I slowly drifted apart and she found a new group of friends. I hadn't discovered who I was.

I always knew what my role was as the oldest child in my family. Because of that, I always had a lot of responsibility placed on my shoulders. When I started junior high, I started meeting new people, and I had new responsibilities as a friend. I felt like an individual. I had my own life, separate from my family. I started recognizing that others were experiencing the same things as I was, and we had more in common than what I had realized before now. The school I attended had fifteen hundred students and about four hundred-fifty were in my grade. I thought that out of all those people, I would find the one single person who was my soul-mate but I never did. I did eventually find a group of people to hang around but nobody I could call a true friend.

Late that summer, my house went up for sale. My parents had always talked about it and I always knew that I would be moving but until my house was actually sold, I kept it in the back of my mind. I had lived in the same city and knew the same people my whole life, and now that I was moving, I didn't know what to think about it.

One day in August, I came home from my friend's house only to find that my house was sold. I didn't know what to feel. Now that someone else bought my house, I had to move. At first, it was no big deal because I did not have a lot of good friends that I was leaving behind anyway. Still, what was I going to do? I called my friend Megan and told her what happened and I started to cry. I usually cry easily over stupid things but this was different. I had to accept the fact that I was changing my life and was going to meet new people. Little did I know that my semi-perfect world was coming to an end, crumbling beneath me, leaving me in an eternal free-fall.

Early that fall I continued to go to the junior high I was enrolled in prior to my house being sold, but my moving date kept getting closer every day. Inside, I was a total wreck, but I couldn't tell anybody. There was no one for me to tell. Every weekend my parents were gone looking for a house to buy while I was at home packing more of my childhood into boxes. The hardest thing about moving was letting go of everything I'd ever known—all the people, places, and things that had defined my world. I had to discover a new me in a new place but it felt more like an ending than a beginning.

I was changing. My personal values, my sense of self, and my outlook on life were taking on greater and greater importance. Yet everywhere I looked, I kept finding people who were mostly interested in impressing others. I desperately wanted to find the perfect friend, someone who cared about the same things I cared about. Mostly, I ended up expecting too much from others and tried to change them to be the way I wanted them to be, and it broke my heart when it didn't work.

My parents never found a house in the location they wanted, so we had no choice but to rent a townhouse. We only moved a mile and a half but still I had to switch schools. I knew that I would be moving again anyway so I didn't bother to attempt meeting new people. My friends at my other school totally broke off all communication with me, abandoning me when I needed them most

I remember a conversation I had with my mother around this time. I was sitting in my room. I spent a lot of time there, often so depressed that I didn't even come out to eat. My mother overheard me crying and came in to see what was wrong. I told her I was crying because I had no friends, that I was depressed and I couldn't stand it. She did her best to reassure me that everything was temporary but it did little to comfort me.

Every day I would sit silently in the same classroom, speaking to no one, while everyone else was talking and laughing. And every day in the lunchroom, everyone would sit with their friends while I sat by myself, in the same place, staring at the wall. I hated it and wouldn't wish the experience on my worst enemy.

By late January, I started feeling more comfortable in my new school. I gradually started making new friends and after a while things didn't seem so bad. In one of my classes, there was a girl named Michelle. We slowly got to know each other and she introduced me to her friends. We started talking and never quit. Finally there was someone who understood me. Someone I could share my thoughts and dreams with. She showed me what it's like to have a real friend and I value her as I have valued no other. After being in seclusion for what seemed like forever, Michelle opened up a new world to me, saving me from the loneliness and depression that I'd known for so long. She came into my life at a point when I really needed a shoulder to lean on. To this day, Michelle is one of the most important people in my life. We have so much to share with each other. She's a very unique person and I hope we'll remain friends, forever.

If my life was a watercolor painting, it was at this point that the colors all bled together and the image faded away because this was the summer my family and I moved to a small town. I'd lived in the suburbs my whole life and now I had to live in a town of two thousand people. It's very different. I had to switch schools again, this time leaving Michelle behind. The hardest thing I've ever had to deal with is change but it is an obstacle that keeps reappearing in my life

Today, most of my close friends are adults. My Aunts Cherie and Shelly are very important to me. They have given me the strength and power to overcome the hardships of being an adolescent. I love them very much. My parents are also idols and role models. I love them very much and don't tell them that enough. I would never be where I am today without the encouragement and determination my parents have given me. Sometimes when I think about my future and what life will be like without my parents and my two aunts, I feel very alone. Yet I know that I'll be able to define a place for myself because of their influence.

In some ways, I am glad that I have had to face the challenge of starting over. It has forced me to look more deeply into myself and has given me a chance to discover myself in ways that probably wouldn't have happened until a later period in my life, if at all. Someday I hope to find out exactly who I am. Meanwhile, I'll push onward through my life, struggling my way through and when my moment of triumph has come, I will know.

GETTING OVER OBSTACLES

Duane Whittaker

In this world everyone is faced with some type of obstacle that enables him or her to do something they want and get to the next level in life. There are many different types of obstacles in the world today. Anything that a person finds challenging can be an obstacle. Most obstacles turn out to be good in the end. Getting over an obstacle can really boost a person's self esteem. It gives a person a sense of pride to know that he or she has gotten by a frightening barrier. If there were no obstacles, the world would be very simple. There would be no challenges and nothing to work for.

When I made the transition from seventh to eighth grade, I was faced with a very difficult obstacle. I had to switch from a public school to a private school. As a seventh grader, I attended Anthony Jr. High. Anthony was the junior high that I always wanted to go to. It was a public school that was 43 percent black and 40 percent white. All of my best friends went to Anthony.

That is one reason why my mother chose to take me out of Anthony for the eighth grade. I was having far too much fun going to school with my friends than I needed to. School started to be more of a social event rather than a learning event. My grades were not good because there were too many extracurricular things going on that had nothing to do with school. For example, instead of participating in class, people would try to run the class. Instead of doing our work, we would sit around, socialize, and gamble. There were a lot of bad influences in the school, which caused me to follow the crowd, and do what everyone else was doing.

At that time in my life I was too young and immature to realize how important it was for me to get a good education. That is when my mother and father decided to send me to a small private school where I would be able to focus on my education. The school I transferred to was called Minnehaha Academy. This school was completely different from Anthony. M.A. was a predominately white school. Not only were the students all white, but they were not from the city. They were all from rich suburban areas such as Minnetonka, Eden Prairie, and Edina. These students were not used to interacting with black students from the city, so I immediately felt like an outsider.

I remember at first I was not the least bit happy about attending this school. I had a very bad attitude. This day was probably my worst ever. I remember a lot of kids looking at me and observing me as if they had never seen a black person before. All the students were very happy and excited to be back in school, except for me. I was depressed. I went home that afternoon, went straight to my room, and cried for several hours. I remember my parents asking me how my first day of school was. My only reply was, "I hate it, I hate it, I hate it!!!"

I did have one friend, Desmond, who went to Minnehaha Academy. My mother and his mother were good friends, and together they decided to send us both to M.A. For the first couple of months, I was very isolated from everyone else. The only person who I would talk to was Desmond. I was always paranoid of what other people were thinking about me. I was always waiting for someone to say something racist to me, to give me a reason to fight, hoping that eventually I would get kicked out of school and get to go back to Anthony. I did run across a few racial problems, and unfortunately I chose to solve them with my fist. My attitude probably made everything worse than it really was. I did not feel like I fit in with the rest of the students.

It took me a very long time to feel accepted. One thing that made it really hard for me was the fact that a lot of my friends still went to Anthony, and they were constantly telling me how much fun they were having. I always felt like I was missing out on everything.

For the first couple of weeks if Desmond was not in one of my classes, I was all alone because the other kids were not very friendly, and they would never ask me to work with them. It really helped me to get through the year at M.A to have one close friend to hang with.

While I was at Minnehaha Academy, I started to really see people's differences. The students at this school were different from me, and to them I was different too. I realized that different was neither good or bad, and no matter how different I was from them, we were all there for the same reason—to get a good education. For a while I had nothing to do with the school besides being there from 7:50 to 2:50 every day.

Things started to change when I started to get myself more involved with the school. I decided that I would play basketball. It was then when I started to feel accepted by the rest of the students. I could finally relate to them in something. I started to gain more friends and be more friendly as a person.

My parents had a lot of influence on me, which helped me to get over this obstacle of not liking the school. They were constantly telling me that my education was very important, and that M.A was an excellent school in terms of education.

While I was at M.A. my biggest obstacle was change—a change in atmosphere, a change in people, a change in my attitude, and a change in my academic future. I can proudly say I conquered my obstacle and successfully finished the year at Minnehaha Academy. During my eighth-grade year, my parents and I both agreed that Minnehaha Academy was an excellent school, but for high school I chose to go to a private school that was more diverse.

A UNIQUE EXPERIENCE IN TODAY'S WORLD

Judith Welliver

For many years we had been renting various homes in the country. We preferred living in the country to living in the city because of the peacefulness and outdoor work one can find there. In September 1990, we moved to the farm place of an old acquaintance. The owner kept a few dry cows there and farmed the land, but other than that we had the place to ourselves. We kept a garden, raised some chickens and goats, and fixed up the house regardless of the fact that it wasn't ours.

Then in the late spring of 1992, the owners decided they wanted the house we were living in. Previously, even before we rented from them, we had helped them out many times—cost free. The house, which had been looking hopeless, now looked as if it had hope at no cost to the owners. Yet, when they decided they could use the house, they told us to get out. We had nowhere to go. For a couple of months we searched for a house, even a house in town, to move into but found nothing. The owners, though, were adamant. We had to move

Finally, after much searching we heard of a farm that was for sale but could be rented, as nobody was living there at the time. The farm was owned by an Amish man, but because of our desperate situation with the owners of the place we were living in, we decided, after some indecision, to move there anyway

This Amish place was in the midst of a fair-sized Amish community, and I assure you, our house especially was more old-fashioned than any other Amish place in the whole community. We had an outdoor toilet while our Amish neighbors had indoor toilets. While we had no running water except the old pump in the kitchen, our neighbors all had running cold water and big reservoirs on their stoves in which hot water was stored. In fact, once when we visited some Amish friends, the wife was fretting because one of their hot water pipes had broken. Her husband was fixing it but she was worrying that it might not be fixed fast enough. Her husband is a machinist and had hooked up a hot-water heater that was run by a gas engine instead of by electricity. I found it very ironic that we, non-Amish and unused to the old fashioned ways, were living in a more old fashioned way than the Amish around us.

We had to live with no electricity, no refrigeration, no running water, and no indoor plumbing for five months. At first, it appeared as if life at that place would be difficult and unreasonable. However, we moved in during mid-July and as the summer passed, life there became more bearable, and we adjusted to the inconvenience of it. For refrigeration we used an extra large icebox or cooler. We filled it with ice and stored the bare minimum of food in it. We rented a locker at the butcher shop in town for our meat. We had a small hand pump at our kitchen sink that served as our only indoor water source. There was also another pump outside at the windmill that we could use. All the water on the place was pumped by the windmill. It pumped water as the wind blew it and filled a reservoir from which we got our water both in the house and outside. There wasn't even a gas pump to back up the windmill. Thankfully, we never ran completely out of water, although we came close to it a couple of times. Whenever we wanted hot water, we had to heat it in a kettle on the stove.

Not having electricity also made a big difference for us. Coming home at night didn't mean flipping on a light switch as we walked through the door. Rather, we first had to use a flashlight to find the matches and then light the lantern before our light came on. We used Coleman gas lanterns and kerosene oil lamps to light our house. I, who had always loved sleeping with a fan on, had to adjust to sleeping in the still quiet on a hot, summer night.

We learned to make do without electric mixers or blenders in the kitchen, and I was unable to play my organ. Going to the bathroom meant going outside to the outhouse, even at night, and taking a bath meant heating water and filling a galvanized, steel tub in the entry. We used a gas run wringer washer or went to the Laundromat when we washed clothes.

I knew, in spite of the absurdity of the living conditions, that because we had nowhere else to go, the situation demanded that we adjust. However, we had little or no help from others. My friends would repeatedly ask or wonder how we could live there. Other people thought we were a little peculiar to live on a place without electricity, and more than once I heard comments about how using lanterns for light must be the equivalent to burning candles (which wasn't true). Regardless of those comments I did adjust.

By the end of the summer, I was beginning to enjoy living there. I liked the hilltop view the place afforded. From our upstairs windows we could see the farms of people who lived two or three miles away. I also enjoyed roaming through the hilly woods and pastures. As for the house, that became bearable too. With the many surrounding shade trees, the house, which was comfortable and roomy to begin with, was also very cool in the summertime. It was a white, two-story house with a large, enclosed front porch and a good-sized back entry room. Throughout, the floors were polished and varnished hardwood. Along with the matching trim and light-blue walls, the house interior had a cozy, authentic look. The kitchen, living room, and five bedrooms were all fair-sized and well arranged. The comfortable atmosphere of the house was a big factor in helping me adjust. The entire building site, which included a large lawn surrounded by a white fence, a barn, and several sheds, all added to the beauty of the place.

With the passing of time I found that I didn't even think twice when I had to go to the outhouse or when I had to light the lantern. I forgot to think about all the missing modern conveniences. By the end of the summer, whenever somebody asked, "How do you like living without electricity?" I would shrug my shoulders and respond, "It's alright. It's no different than living with electricity once your used to it."

In December, we found another place to move to, so we again had electricity and all other modern conveniences. However, I was just the slightest bit regretful to leave that place since after adjustment I had enjoyed the tranquillity there. Although I lived in conditions that are unthinkable to most people in the United States by today's modern standards, I found that living in such a manner is not impossible or harsh. I still think

we may as well use and appreciate the modern conveniences that others have invented for the benefit of mankind, but I now know that living without them can also be possible and peaceful once such a lifestyle is accepted.

I just want to add an epilog to this story. I had that living experience in the summer and fall of 1992. We found another place to move to in December 1992. In June I finished high school, and last fall I moved to Minneapolis to begin further schooling at the University of Minnesota. That is why I now live in the city rather than in the country.

ALCOHOL AND DRUGS

for the country's
fixed. While there
vices to assist street
en table, her sitting,
ock, the interrogation began
me control over his future
behavior set in
ptured
their arms
here in
when he hit me. So
chair and the kitchen table
lying in the hammock, th

ALCOHOL AND DRUGS

The three young people in this section write about experiences with alcohol and other drugs. In Situ Angst writes about the night her mother found out about her drug use, her treatment, and what she believes will happen in her life now that she has been through this. She has hope, and after we finish reading her essay, we do too. She reveals the self-knowledge that comes from all the work of getting off drugs. She is wonderfully realistic and admits that some days are still harder than others. When we finish her story we are tempted to give her a call to wish her luck.

Kelly Godfrey opens her essay: "My head began to spin as I stumbled into the dark room." She takes us through one drunken night when she is almost raped. As a result of this she comes to realize that she has to stop abusing alcohol and other drugs. It is a short, powerful essay that should be required reading for young people everywhere.

The final essay in this section is by Andrea, who decides not to drink alcohol. It costs her her closest friends. She ends her essay by letting us know how hopeful she feels about her life now and about how the lives of her drinking former friends have turned out. This story is one of strength in the face of that powerful force: peer pressure, and it is also about the positive result that can come from holding on to our convictions.

CHOICES

Andrea Anderson

Growing up in the nineties is a hard thing to do. The peer pressure is worse than ever before. I think the biggest pressure is to drink alcohol.

This is my first year of high school. Being a sophomore is hard. You want to fit in with your class, but you also want to fit in with the upperclassman. It seems like the only way to fit in is to drink.

At the beginning of this school year my life was going great. It was the swim season, I was on student council, and I had all the friends I needed. It didn't seem like alcohol was a problem. The friends I had were concerned about their sports and school work just like me. Nobody ever thought about drinking.

Throughout the year the pressure to do alcohol increased. You couldn't find a party where there wasn't alcohol or where people weren't drinking. My friends started going to these parties. They soon started drinking. I didn't want to go, because drinking is the one thing that I'm strictly against. My friends didn't understand me. They thought it was fun to go out and get drunk every weekend. My relationship with my friends started decreasing. While I was spending more time with sports and school and trying to excel, they were trying to figure out what parties had the most alcohol. I tried talking to my friends about their drinking. I told them that they either had to stop their drinking or stop being friends with me. My friends chose the alcohol. They were the closest friends that I had. I had known them for a long time. I couldn't believe that they thought drinking was more important than our friendship.

As the school year went on, I found new friends that had the same interests and morals I did. Now everything is going great again. I've kept a 3.2

grade point average all year. It's golf season now and I'm still on student council. While my life is going uphill, my "old" friends' lives are going downhill. They're falling off the honor rolls and some of them have quit their sports they've been in all their lives. I'm glad that I found myself and got on with my life. It was the hardest thing in the world to let go of my friends, but I knew I had to do it. I think you should always do what's right for yourself and what will be right for you in the long run. It might seem bad at first, but it will always improve.

INFLUENCES
In Situ Angst

I believe that we are beings who are constantly changing, from the time we are babies, to the time that we are very old. For instance, I am in no way the same person that I was last year at this time. Since I also believe that every experience in our lives adds to the person we become, if you were to ask me who I am today and what made me this way, I would probably have to start with my most recent experiences and move backward.

The most recent major experience that shaped my life has been drug treatment. Obviously if one were to go through treatment and chose to let it work, they would become a very changed person. I had to change my life to make it work.

April 12, 1993 is a date I will never forget. It was the night that triggered the change in my life. The way my mom discovered my drug use is almost ironic in a sick way. Here I had been using drugs for five years, quite heavily for one of those years, and she found out by simply reading one coincidental letter out of the myriad I write. I had been writing this ill-fated letter to a friend in St. Cloud. I left my room for some reason and decided to go downstairs. My mom thought that I was in my room and went in to talk to me. She glanced down at the notebook on my bed and the word marijuana "jumped" out at her. She went on to read the rest of the notebook, which was my journal at the time, and discovered some very unpleasant things. One of which was that I had been using some drugs.

She covertly called my dad, told him of her new-found knowledge, and got me on the phone with her and him. She looked me in the eye and said, "Amy, I want you to tell me the truth about something."

I was really stoned at the time and she looked really funny because she looked like she was trying to be really serious. She did not find me nearly as funny as I did her. She was not only trying to be serious, she was really serious. The questions and accusations that flew after her initial comments however, sobered me up pretty quickly. I was angry with her because I felt she had invaded my right to privacy. (I still maintain that I had hidden my notebook under my bed and there is no way she could have seen what I was writing unless she was looking for it.) There were also a tremendous amount of family issues that had been going on for years—so many issues that I could write ten essays about them. But this to me, seemed like one last injustice that they were trying to force on me.

In retrospect, I have no idea what this injustice was, but really, when I think of how crazy my thinking was until they came and got me, I have to laugh. I even had an escape route all planned out. I was going to go to the bank and withdraw all my money, leave a hundred dollars for the cost of my car (that would have more than covered it) on the doorstep of my house, and drive East until I had no more money for gas. I'm not really sure what I would have done then. Maybe just sat around and smoked weed.

I did run away the next day, but it was not nearly as dramatic as my dreams. But then you must remember, I had to get to the bank and get home to get my car before I could put any of this plan into action. Fortunately, my mom put a stop to my ideas, because when I went home to take my car, she had pulled all the hoses out so that it was not driveable.

Anyhow, my father ended up flying home from Colorado where he lived, and he and my mother came and took me from school. It was the beginning of the day. I didn't have any idea that they were coming for me, and I had no idea where I was going.

That, however, is not the main focus of my essay. The main focus is what got me into treatment, what happened there, and how it has changed me now.

Typically, I didn't realize that I had a problem, why should I? Everyone around me seemed to be keeping up with my use. Of course in retrospect,

I realize this is a false notion, but at the time I saw nothing wrong with what I was doing.

I had gone for so long with one behavior being ingrained in me that I had no idea how to act when it was taken away. I had grown up using or idealizing the using lifestyle. There I was, a little kid in elementary school, seeing the older kids who seemed to have all this power and sophistication and, well, the age, that I wanted so desperately.

I then went on to junior high—the natural progression of things—and began to work on getting that recognition as an individual. For some odd reason, to me drugs represented individuality. I saw using them as being free and uninhibited. I also saw them as being very powerful, and I believed that if I could control that power, I could finally be happy. That power, of course, ended up controlling me. By the time I was in high school I was slowly letting go or forgetting about a lot of my dreams. Dreams like doing well in school, going to college, becoming a professional musician, even making it to my eighteenth birthday.

My junior year I dropped all of my academic classes but two, enriched English and enriched history, and took all art classes. I thought that this would give me good reason to stay in school. It didn't, apparently, because if I hadn't been put into treatment, I doubt if I would have passed my junior year.

An intervention is what concerned by-standers in a user's life get together and do. They lovingly and nonjudgmentally inform the user in question that he or she has a problem and that they, the concerned by-standers, are placing the user in the care of "loving" and "non-judgmental" professionals.

Well, after my parents abducted me from school on the fifth day of my sojourn from home they didn't have much time to do an intervention on me since we were on the way to the treatment center. And though I'm sure it started out right, it sure didn't end up very "loving" or "non-judgmental."

Many people go into treatment very angry, especially right after an intervention like I had. I must be the exception to that generalization. I found my situation more humorous than anything else. I remember the counselor telling me over and over that it was all right to be angry, in fact it was good let angry emotions out. I sat there nodding my head and thinking, what do I have to be angry about? All they want me to do is sit here, watch videos, and play cards eight hours a day instead of school, which I hate. Plus I get credit for school?

This sounded like a great deal. Sure the idea of not being able to talk to anyone would be hard. But I was an incredibly independent person, and though I would miss my friends, I didn't especially need them for anything. I would be able to talk to them and go back to hanging out with them as soon as I got out.

I soon found out that my idea about going back to the old life, even though I would be a supposedly changed person, was wrong. I actually had to find out that a lot of my old ideas were wrong and had to be changed. I would find out that changing one's old ideas and beliefs are what it's all about.

I was very resistant to treatment, but once again not in the way most people are. I viewed it as a joke and intellectualized the whole first half to the point where I didn't make sense to myself. I didn't especially care that I was there, and took the view that I would stay sober for all of treatment and see what it did for me. I could not, however, see a life without drugs at this point.

I don't know when the turning point came, but it was right around my first A.A. meeting. I had been skipping all of my A.A. meetings with a group of kids in my group at treatment. We never got caught, but one Monday night I decided to try attending just for the fun of it. I didn't want to make it all the way through treatment with out going to a single A.A. meeting. I don't know what happened in that room that night, what it was about what the people said; all I know is that it was really cool. All I know is that it changed my attitude. I realized finally that my life could change, I could recapture my dreams and become something. I also knew that I could never go back. It felt really good to let that past go. I was what I had idealized as a child, and I now know that it wasn't all that great.

In conclusion, I cannot say that I don't have struggles occasionally with my sobriety. I am bipolar, a manic depressive's politically correct phrase, so that doesn't make it any easier. I have changed so much in such a short period of time. So much has been both taken and given to me so abruptly, I have a lot of inner turmoil. All I can say is that, like any other experience, treatment has changed me. I hope for the better.

WHEN THE PARTY'S OVER

Kelly Godfrey

My head began to spin as I stumbled into the dark room. I tripped over something on the floor, probably a person from the party downstairs, and landed on a bed. The second I closed my eyes, I felt like I was flying. It was a frightening feeling, and there was nothing I could do to make it stop. I was out of control. Regaining my composure was impossible, though I struggled relentlessly to do so. I buried my face in a pillow and hoped I would fall asleep and wake up sober the next morning. I don't even remember how many different drugs I'd taken or how much alcohol I drank that night. Over and over in my head, I pleaded with God to take that helpless feeling away. A sickening pain was growing inside my body as I swore up and down that I would never drink or do any drugs ever again. Then it got so bad I was sure I was dying, so I just lay there, waiting.

The next thing I knew someone was in bed with me, trying to undo my belt. I was so disoriented I forgot what to do. I knew there was something that might get me out of that situation, but I couldn't think of what it was. So, I just lay there staring up at the boy. The darkness of the room swallowed up his face when I tried to distinguish whether or not I knew him. The forceful persistence of his hands on my body suddenly snapped me back into reality. It was as if God struck me sober, and I found the strength to push the drunk stranger off me.

My heart fluttered as I ran into the bathroom where I slammed and locked the door behind me. The bright lights in the bathroom hurt my eyes, and I felt dizzy. Grabbing onto the sink for support, I realized I was in front of a huge mirror with my own reflection staring back at me. My face was ghostly pale, and there were dark circles beneath my bloodshot eyes. I looked as horrible as I felt. Unable to stand the pathetic sight of myself, I collapsed on the cool tiles of the floor and began to cry. The tears continued until I was too exhausted to stay awake any longer.

The next day I awoke to the worst headache I'd ever had. Remembering the events from the previous night only made it worse. I had never been so angry in my life. Not so much at the guy who had tried to take advantage of me, but more at myself for being so careless. I've often heard stories about girls being raped while intoxicated, but I always assumed they'd asked for it. I was wrong. I didn't want to be sexually involved with someone I didn't know, and I hated the thought of people using others for sex. But I had to claim responsibility for getting myself into that situation.

Through this awful experience I realized that life is tough enough without putting myself into risky situations, When your mind is altered it's hard to comprehend what you're doing. I've learned from my mistake and consider myself very lucky because it could have been a fatal one. With the high risk of sexually transmitted diseases in the world today, all of us should be use our brains and play it safe. If we don't watch out for each other, the problems we have now will only get bigger.

PEER PRESSURE

t for the country's
ixed. While there
ervices to assit street
en table, her sitting,
ock, the interrogation began
me control over his future
tical behaviors set in
uptured
their arms I
always so much here in
when he hit me. I'd
and he would
lying in the hammock, th

PEER PRESSURE

It is not surprising that many young people who entered this contest decided to write about peer pressure. In these five essays we see the response of each person to this ever present problem for adolescents. An anonymous young man opens his story "Making the Right Choice" with the words:

"In my lifetime I've overcome many things: being scared of the dark, scared of the water, scared to die, scared to live. I still haven't overcome the last one and here's why."

We know from that opening how serious is the situation of our young people. This writer manages to escape the temptations and suggestions of his "friends" and to feel better for it, but it leaves him with fear and sadness.

Tyane includes these lines in her beginning poem: "Life will never stop/because you are broken-hearted . . ." She goes on to describe how she fell in love with a boy named Mike, how she gave up all her friends for him, and how he eventually left her. Her grades dropped, she fought with her family, and she "kept a knife in my drawer just in case." She finally turned to writing to relieve some of her pain and in the end of the essay, she concludes, in favor of love. No matter how much she has been hurt she won't give up on it. This is a moving testament to the fact that what may seem like an inconsequential break up of a first love, can mean so much to the young people involved.

Brea writes about dealing with the despair of being young, exposed to drugs, suicide, and her decision to ask a friend to choose between drugs or their friendship. Again, Brea asks us to take her seriously.

Tyler Shaw goes into fascinating detail about what he feels when he steals something from an exhibition. He describes with clarity his reaction after the theft, being caught and how it changed him. It is, in the end, a hopeful, upbeat story.

Alicia McMurphy says, near the end of her essay: "I thought, to be cool you would have to get into trouble, steal, and lie. Now I know that's not true." She takes us into her confidence and describes all the things she did that got her sent to juvenile center and in serious trouble. Again, though, as with Tyler's essay, we feel she has come out of it.

In the final essay, an anonymous young woman really writes advice to young people on how to stay out of all this trouble. She tells us how she stopped worrying about the crowd and simply found pride in being herself. "When I found pride, I found the answer to surviving as an African-American." This is an important story, one that may make many young people think hard about who they are in this world.

MAKING THE RIGHT CHOICE

Anonymous

In my lifetime I've overcome many things: being scared of the dark, scared of the water, scared to die, scared to live. I still haven't overcome the last one and here's why.

When I got into the seventh grade I met "my lifelong friend." We talked and did things together, and we were happy with what we had. His goal was something I didn't want—major popularity, a thing he really cared about. We were still friends but a month later things changed.

I began growing physically and mentally. I broadened my interests and gained more knowledge. I read a lot which is something I love. "Reading's for nerds. Why do you read when you don't have to?" The comments were coming from my "best friend." So I decided that I'd do something he liked; smoking was the thing "cool" people did. Drinking was for the "losers" and the "cool" people. So I experimented with all this stuff. I did not take a liking to the smoking but this was "my best friend" so I wanted to please him.

Another thing he liked to do was make fun of foreigners and people who are different than white people. This is stuff I hate because I'm a believer in equal rights, even though this world isn't.

I tried all this fun and didn't take a liking to it, but this was "my best friend" so I tried to please him.

My kind of music style is Jimi Hendrix, The Doors, and guitar. But when I was with my "friend" I never mentioned it. The one time he saw it he made fun of me calling me a "nigger lover" and calling it "nigger rock". This went on for the rest of the seventh grade, along with planned changes so he could be with the "popular people," pranking "nerds" and other activities I didn't approve of.

I quit smoking. I didn't really talk to him any more. Things were better. I started showing my style and got noticed for it. I still don't care for popularity, but that's a different story. We just went our separate ways and now I'm happy—happy to live the way I want to.

HOW LONG IS FOREVER?

Tyane

> One life to live
> is what happens to be said,
> life still goes on
> while you pretend to be dead.
> One broken heart and the game begins,
> but if you stop loving then everything ends.
> Hawaii is yours will always come back to you,
> but with what never was, there's nothing you can do.
> Life will never stop because you are broken-hearted,
> and it'd be a shame not to finish something you've already started.
> Never be afraid to love or live again.
> A heart can break,
> but in time it will mend.

I wrote this poem in order to express my feelings to others, or just so I'd know exactly what I'm thinking. Poems also help me get through very difficult times when I really have no idea what to do. What you just read took me three years of my life to finally figure out.

Have you ever seen or been around someone where you know right away, that's the person you want to be with for a very long time, maybe even forever? It's funny how those "forever" turns into a year, or month, and for some people, may be only a week or so. One "forever" goes and another one comes along, but I'm going to tell you about one in particular that almost broke me.

Imagine your first year of high school. Nothing could be more perfect. I had a strong group of friends, sports were going well, and of course, there were so many new guys to choose from. Then it happened. Our group expanded, and out of nowhere was Mike. Mike wasn't the best looking guy, but with his charming personality, he could win anyone over. Lisa, one of the girls in my group, already had her eye on him, and so did a few others. Therefore, I tried keeping more than a friendship with him out of my mind. Then it started. The dreams of him kept coming. Every time he walked by my stomach started paining, and those eyes, kept staring. It came to the point where I would have to wake myself up in order to concentrate on something else.

I thought this was just an ordinary "school-girl crush," but the truth is I was becoming obsessed with him. Later Lisa started going out with him, yet he would still flirt with me. I told myself to let it be, no guy is worth a friendship, right? The more I tried to resist Mike the stronger my feelings were. No longer was he Mike, just a guy we hung around. Mike became my world, my life. He would come to me about problems with Lisa, and I found myself giving him false information just so they would break up. I also ended up telling Lisa things that Mike was doing, or saying about her, to me.

Eventually Lisa and Mike broke up, and Lisa was devastated. She would come to me with thoughts of suicide, and all I could do was think about how Mike was feeling. He and I became very close, that we were beyond friendship. I abandoned my two very close friends of our little group, Jessica and Le, but as long as Mike and I were progressing, I didn't care. Just then Mike started going out with another girl, who was more my acquaintance than a friend. I started to tell Mike things about this girl that were half true and half very exaggerated.

Mike began to trust in me, and started to lose interest in this girl as quickly as he had found it. We would hang out more often; then finally, we were a couple. I had already fallen in love with this guy, so of course I'd do anything for him. I betrayed Lisa, who at the time, told me she didn't care that we were going out, but I could see the hurt in her eyes. How come I didn't listen to those eyes and to my heart? The only reason I can think of is that I was in it for myself. I started to hurt a lot of people, but it didn't matter to me as long as Mike was there. Lisa tried to warn me about him—that he would leave me just as fast as he left the others. I just laughed, yet not in a very confident way. Why would he leave me? I asked myself. He promised me forever and that's how long he's planning to stay. But the doubt still lingered in my mind.

Then it happened. Mike and I broke up, but more than that I almost ruined a lot of friendships, (Lisa, Jessica, Le, Nina, and me), that were supposed to last. Like I said, Mike was my life, and he basically controlled me. If he told me to be with him and no one else, that's what I would do. I barely saw my friends anymore, and even though Lisa said she was over it, I knew it hurt her to see us together. Lisa began to drift away until we saw her only on some occasions. Maybe it wasn't my fault. It might have been bound to happen. I mean, in high school don't your friendships change? Nevertheless, I did help it along and never thought twice about it.

After Mike and I were through I spent a lot of time hiding. I was hiding from the pain, the truth, and myself. But my hiding wasn't obvious. Sometimes I couldn't even tell. My sports started to be my life so much that the only time I really saw my friends was during lunch. When people asked me about Mike, or if I saw him hand-in-hand with someone else, my first response was, I really don't give a damn. The truth was that deep down it was tearing me apart. I wanted to be that new someone Mike was holding hands with. Then I realized that I just felt so alone, and all I really wanted was to be somebody's new someone.

It felt like I was trapped and no matter what I did things just kept getting worse. My grades dropped, I would lash out at my family. Sports meant nothing to me anymore, and neither did my life. Suicide wasn't the furthest from my mind, even though I knew I could never go through with it. Yet sometimes when I was alone in my room, I would just sit and wonder if anyone would really care if I was gone. In fact I kept a knife in my drawer just in case.

I knew I couldn't go on like that and I had to let it out, to tell someone. My only problem was that there was no one to tell it to. That's when I decided I had to know exactly how I was feeling, and so I began to write.

The words just started to pour out, and when I reread what was written, for the first time I felt my life getting back to whatever normal was.

Then it happened. Just as I was starting to get back on my feet, Mike decided he wanted to come back, and I said yes. I had to, I just had to know if our feelings were for real. More than that though, I needed to feel loved again. Mike showed me things and had me feeling ways I never thought possible, and I had to feel that once more. He really never was flawless, still there was the caring and sweetness in his eyes. And in those eyes was the person I wanted as my "forever." Things went fine for awhile, but again Mike went back to his old ways, and this time I knew it was good-bye.

After our second breakup I had the support I really needed. Even though Mike hurt me beyond any pain I've ever endured, he also did something for me that I don't think anyone else could have. He helped me grow as a person, especially with relationships. He also got me to realize who my true friends were. No matter what I put people through, my two best friends, Jessica and Le, never left my side, and they're still here with me today.

Love is not something you'll just wake up with one morning. It takes a lot of work and commitment, and yes, sometimes life really hurts. After all of this I thought I would never love or live for myself again, but now things are very different. I know even if the next person I'm with doesn't turn out to be "Mr. Right," at least I'll always have my friends who aren't going anywhere.

Through my poems I have learned no matter how much I've been hurt, or how hard I thought it was to love again, it will only ruin you, if you ever stop loving.

ADOLESCENCE: A STAGE IN LIFE
Brea

"April is the cruelest month, broaden lilacs out of the dead land mixing memory and desire stirring dull roots with the spring rain."

The Waste Land [1922]
— T.S Elliot

Adolescence is like a lilac bush: it blooms with intense beauty for a transitory period of time and then slowly it fades away leaving "dull roots" in spring rain. Adolescence is a complicated time of searching for answers amid the questions of identity and self-discovery that surround our complex lives. There are times when we wish that we could give up and end it all; those are the times when we tore the beauty of that lilac bush. Despair takes root and chokes out the flower, adopting the waste land for its home. Adolescence can be a time of growth and re-discovery, but it also can be a time of stagnation, self-denial, and darkness, and, like T. S. Elliot's "April," it can be the "cruelest month" of one's life.

At this time in my enigmatic life, many problems have arisen with many of my peers that I never thought could or should appear at such an early age in our lives. Problems such as drugs, suicide, and experimentation encircle our lives like the earth encircles the sun. So then, I ask myself: Is there anything that I can do to stop myself from falling into that darkness, into the deep? At this point I realize there is no escape from adolescence, except the eternal, and I am not willing to go that route.

I have been subjected to these pressures along with many of my peers. Some have rejected them, but the majority have accepted the situation. I once had a best friend who had so much potential. She was smart, pretty, and funny. When she got into high school, she changed drastically. She started drinking, then smoking, and eventually she got into pot and other drugs. I did not want to be around her anymore, and it tore me apart.

I do not want this to be just another sad, sad, sob story about someone in the inner-city who got into the wrong crowd but that best friend of mine is now dead. She was only fifteen years old. These kinds of problems should not happen to someone who is at the very peak of her life.

The pressures in my life are not drugs or alcohol, and because of this I find myself alone, enclosed in a small place, locked away from all human contact. There is no best friend in my life today. It seems like there is no one left who has not already fallen into the native trips of adolescence. I remove myself from others for fear of becoming like them or becoming part of their activities. So many of my friends have been swallowed up, and I am afraid that I may get hurt again, so I never get close. It is my choice to separate myself; it was a way to forget and eventually to overcome my fears. But somehow I feel that this is hurting me more.

My friend got into high school and found out that she could not handle it, so she then turned to synthetic pleasures. She kept saying, "You can't get hooked just by using it once." She placed a wall between us. I tried to help her, but she would not listen. When she died, I felt so guilty. I thought that it was all my fault that I could not convince her to stop. I felt this also because I made her choose: Either the drug goes or I go. My mother told me of a situation similar to my own experience, and then I knew that there was nothing that I could have done; I had tried my hardest. At this point, I know that I have overcome this situation, and even though I know that there will be more similar situations to come, I look on the future with an open mind and heart. I know that my parents will be there to help me understand and will help me cope.

Until a week ago my thoughts on adolescence were that it was just something that you must go through to reach adulthood, and that at the end of adolescence is the end of all problems. We look forward to the future with open minds contrary to most adults' thoughts of reminiscences and regret.

One week ago I went to a funeral. It was the funeral of a childhood friend's mother. She had commuted suicide. Now I know that adolescence is just another excuse to put the blame on because all the "problems" that accompany adolescence follow you throughout your life.

This stage in our lives is harder to get through now than it was thirty years ago. I am afraid for the future and for my children. Life should not be like this, and I think it is time for us, this generation, to start taking responsibility for things no matter whose fault it was. Because if we do not, who will? We are only borrowing our children's future and their world.

GROWING FROM EXPERIENCE

Tyler Shaw

In April when I was in seventh grade, our school had planned a trip to the Festival of Nations, which is a convention of many different exhibitions about races and nationalities. They have crafts and foods from around the world to buy and show.

I was very excited about this trip because I had been there previously with my family and I had really enjoyed it. I walked around with some of my good friends for most of the time there. But we got separated in a crowd, so I went off with some other kids who I was not that good of friends with. I figured it was better to go with them than be alone.

While I was with these kids, we would run around and cause little disturbances among the people. We then met up with some kids who said they had just stolen some necklaces from an African exhibit. We asked them where it was so we could check it out. They brought us over there and showed us how to do it. At first I just watched the kids I was with because it didn't feel right. After seeing all the kids doing it, and getting away with it, I decided to give it try.

I walked up to the stand and took a necklace down from the hook, like the others had. I then casually walked amongst a big crowd of people surrounding the booth, and walked nervously away. Waiting not to far away was the kid who shared this idea with the rest of us. I showed him the necklace that I ever so cautiously had walked off with. He congratulated me, as if it was something to be proud of. Because of his congratulation, I began to think it was something to be proud of. So, I joyfully showed it to all of my peers. When I had tired of showing the necklace, I went back to get another one, so I could show it off all over again. In that fury of pride and acceptance, I forgot my true values, which I had usually lived up to until then. Even on the way home I showed off my tainted prizes to the kids on my bus.

When I got home I still thought nothing of what had occurred that day. I was so lost that I even showed my parents the necklaces. I made up a lame story to cover up for what I had just done. The next day and many days after I wore the necklaces to school and wherever I went.

One day when I had stayed home sick, I got a call from a not-too-good friend who I still hung around with. He called to tell me that the school was doing an investigation on the kids who had stolen necklaces. Hearing that made me feel worse than I had ever felt before. I felt so alone and trapped because I didn't want to tell my parents, and I knew that I was going to get caught. There was no way out.

I turned it over in my mind all weekend until Monday morning when the principal at my school announced that anyone involved in the stealing could turn themselves in and get a slightly reduced punishment. I had heard that I wasn't on the list of suspects, so I didn't come voluntarily forward. Later that day during class the phone rang. The principal wanted me down in the office for something, but I knew deep down that it was over. I waited impatiently next to the principal's office until he called me in. He told me that he had heard from anonymous sources that I was involved with the theft of some crafts from the Festival of Nations. I denied it, but he said that I did it. So I gave in.

The moment I said that I had done it I felt better. I felt some weight lift from my chest, but it wasn't over. He asked for my phone number so we could talk to my parents about this. I was scared, but felt relieved that they would finally know the truth. He spoke to them briefly then handed the phone over to me. That was the toughest conversation I had ever had with my parents. They were angry as any normal parent would be. They said that we would talk about it later. I dreaded going home that day, but I did it any way. They asked me what I was thinking and questioned why I was so proud when I had showed the necklaces to them. I said I didn't know to both of the questions.

After about a week all the people who were involved in the theft were called down to the school office to discuss our consequences. They said that no matter how much we stole, stealing is stealing and that we were all going to get the same punishment. Except the people who had turned themselves in only got eight hours of community service and had to return the stolen items. But the other kids that didn't confess (which included me) got twelve hours of community service and also had to return the stolen items. We were all put on probation against participating in all school activities, including dances and field trips until January 1 of the following year, when our behavior would be evaluated by school officials.

I completed my community service at the local library, which wasn't very fun. But I didn't expect it to be in the first place. I was also grounded by my parents for a month, which seemed like an eternity, considering I did something every day up until I was grounded.

Over the summer I started to hang around with a new group of kids that weren't involved in the stealing incident. There was no outside pressure from them to do something I didn't want to do. Before the end of that school year I told a teacher that I would change and mature over the summer. After he heard that he laughed because he didn't believe that I could change. This past year I have made myself go down the right path. I also felt that stealing was not the kind of life I wanted for myself. I didn't like having to prove myself to people, so I decided just to be me.

IN AND OUT OF TROUBLE

Alicia McMurphy

Hello, my name is Alicia McMurphy, and I'm almost fourteen. I'll be fourteen in May. All my problems started in the summer of '92. I met a friend who did a lot of skipping school and was into lots of violence. But I didn't know she did these things. Well I got mixed up in the wrong crowd. She got me to smoke cigarettes and drink. After awhile we started to steal cars and it was like I was in my own little world. I was the one in control of myself and only myself. Nobody could tell me what to do and that's the way I liked it.

Well, after being in Juvenile Center all the time I got sick of it. So when I got out all I would do was get into more trouble and had an assault record at the age of twelve. My life was really going down the drain, but I didn't care at all. It felt like I could never stop getting into trouble so I didn't even try or put any effort into changing the way I was acting. My mom sent me to my aunt's for a month to see if I could change my act. My aunt is a very strong woman and doesn't take no for an answer. I thought I would have gotten out of all this trouble, living with her. But even this arrangement failed. When we were living together I got taken back to her house by the police once for causing trouble uptown.

After a month had passed I was still getting into trouble, but it was time for me to go home and I was so happy. The first thing I did when I got home was steal another car. My mom tried to put me in a program. In this program they paid me to be good. It worked for awhile. Then I just started up again.

Six months went by and I was still on the same program, but I was doing a little better. I wasn't in as much trouble as when I had started, which was good. I felt that a miracle might have happened.

They finally took me off the program so I could try it on my own. I stole another car and then was put on house arrest. On house arrest you can't go anywhere, see any friends, and you have to be good or they'll lock you up for awhile at a girls home. I got dropped off at school and picked up from school by my mom. I had to wear a black box around my ankle and the police knew where I was at all times. It wasn't fun at all.

November rolled around and I was still getting into trouble. By this time I was really sick of it. I had to spend Thanksgiving Day in Juvenile Center. I felt like nobody even cared or they weren't doing their best to get me out. When I got out that weekend I went to my Grandma's house to think things over and to try to get out of all the trouble I was in. I went home a week later with a different attitude, but I still didn't care.

I moved a couple weeks later, away from my friend who was getting me into all this trouble. My mom didn't want me hanging around her, but I would sneak around with her and make up lies to cover it. My mom finally found out, and that was the end of it. That day we gave each other's stuff back, sat and laughed at all the good times we had, and were wondering if we would ever see each other again. But we never did.

Now, I am clean and I haven't got into trouble since last summer. I've been going to school, home on time, and listening to my mom. My life is finally the way I wanted it to be.

I thought, to be cool you would have to get into trouble, steal, and lie. Now I know that's not true. Sometimes I'll drink or I'll have a cigarette just to remember my best friend. We were very close, but now I have my life together, while she's still getting into trouble. I'm proud of myself and so is my mom. Just last week I got a letter in the mail. I have to go to court April 26, 1994 to get off of probation. The judge I have is also proud of me and I'm glad to get out of all that trouble. I don't want to be working at McDonald's or Burger King. I want a good career and I want to make good money for a family some day instead of getting into trouble and being in jail all the time. I have accomplished something great for myself instead of doing it for friends.

OBSTACLES OVERCOME: FINDING ME

Anonymous

Pride is a word that is the basis of my everyday life. It gives me courage to overcome any obscure obstacles that come my way and it also gives me the will to want to do the best I can to succeed—not only for the bettering of the world, but also for my own self assurance. To many, pride brings fear into their hearts, disillusionment to their souls, and discomfort to their spirits because they lose sight of what pride really means.

That is what happened to me. I thought that pride was a cynical view that people had of themselves. In my opinion, people who said that they had pride in themselves were trying to hide something wicked about themselves that they didn't want anyone to find out about. So they put on this "I'm confident of myself" act to make people believe that they had themselves together. I, for one, did not want to be known as a shallow, egotistical person. I wanted everyone to think that I was the type of person that would always see to everyone else's needs and wants before I even dared to consider myself. The truth was I didn't take pride in myself and therefore had to seek it out by doing things for other people. But instead of helping me, it showed what a shallow person I really was.

I know what it is like to always follow the crowd because I couldn't think for myself. I know what it is to think that I'm a nobody because my hair wasn't as long as "Tanya's" or my clothes weren't as nice as "Clarice's." It's hard not fitting in with the "in" crowd because you feel as if you're less of a person or nobody is going to like you because you don't hang out with all the popular kids. That all comes from not having pride in yourself.

After years of living in everyone's shadow, I came to grips with the reality that I am a unique individual that will no longer compromise who I am for the approval of others. As long as I have the approval of myself, that's the only approval I need.

There will always be those that will pressure you to compromise who you are to become like them. Misery loves company. Anyone who would have you sell yourself short of living out your full potential is a miserable person who only wants to drag you down the road of self pity with them so they don't have to take the journey alone. Those are the people that I had to rid myself of in order to be who I am: a proud, African-American female who will not be cut short of the American dream because I deserve the best.

Overcoming the lifestyle of self-pity, dictatorship, and manipulation is extremely difficult. But if you're willing to tap into "you," nothing is as impossible as it seems. When living the life where pride is void and dictatorship rules, you become subject to others. Selfish attitudes begin to rule your decisions. Thinking on your own ceases like a river that runs dry after a hot July. But you don't have to live that kind of life. It's all up to you. The only thing you have to do is believe in who you are and have pride in yourself, and then everything else will fall in place.

As I said before, it isn't easy coming out of the "pity closet", but once you're out, you experience unspeakable joy because you are finally being who you are. I found out that pride is a word that sums up the feelings of joy, peace, love, and prosperity. I found out that with pride in myself, nothing is impossible.

Being African-American, I must have pride to succeed in life. Unless I am aware of who I am, nothing is possible for me to obtain. When I found pride, I found the answer to surviving as an African-American. It's not who I can get to accept me as a minority, it's who I can make realize that I'm proud to be a minority. Many obstacles, maybe more than the norm, come my way as being who I am—but with pride I have been able to overcome every one. Yes, there will be times where obstacles may seem insurmountable, but I can now face them with a positive attitude and with a belief that I will come out victorious in the end.

BODY IMAGE

for the country's
ixed. While there
vices to assit street
n table, her sitting,
ock, the interrogation began
ne control over his future
~~ional behavior set in a~~
~~uptured~~
~~their arms I~~
~~always so much~~ bite in
~~themselves~~
~~when he hit me. I'd~~
~~between and he would hit~~ table
lying in the hammock, th

BODY IMAGE

Considering the ways young people are changing physically, the following three essays should not surprise us. At the same time that their bodies are going through profound transformations, there is an almost unbearable emphasis on how they look, what clothes they wear, how much they weigh.

In the first essay, "Slim Chances," an anonymous young woman takes us through a harrowing account of the things he did to lose weight—the pills, the diets, etc. She says:

"Why did I do it? Why do I still have urges? Because I didn't want to be judged badly, because I didn't want to be the joke, because even though it's wrong, I'd rather be judged for size four rather than shunned for my old size eleven."

Kristin Schmitz takes us on a similar journey through her various attempts to lose weight from fourth grade until the end of her sophomore year in high school. It is a painful struggle, and while we are pleased she is happy with her success at losing weight, we are still left to wonder, as we were with the preceding young woman, whether we are pushing kids too hard to be too skinny.

Finally, for a light touch, we are treated in "Getting Started" to a young man's attempts to be short and play basketball. Appropriately, this is a short essay about the problem of being short. It is a gem.

SLIM CHANCES

Anonymous

Maybe I'm a paranoid person, maybe I tend to exaggerate things, or maybe what I think about is true and that's why I sometimes feel as though I won't make it in a world that expects too much. But if by chance, I am wrong, then why die? It seems in my mind that all skinny people are portrayed as successful people with whom we should model ourselves after. Why do I feel like I need to be skinny in order to find acceptance? And why does being overweight linger in my mind, and why does it echo in my mind that being any way but skinny is a bad omen for my whole life?

The feelings of fear and obsession that society perpetuates drove me over the edge. The image projected placed me in the middle of a helpless and lonely circle. This same society put the standard of thinness among us and told me how I should be no matter how I got there, and told everyone else how to perceive me depending on the outcome of my struggles.

As a result of this mendacity, I began to seek thinness no matter what price I had to pay—my never-ending game of tug-of-war between who I was and who I wanted to be through the eyes of others.

It began with a simple diet in eighth grade, to eventual skipping of as many meals as I could, without being caught. After entering high school. I got involved in activities and found more independence without super-vision. Losing weight was a looming shadow that hung more frequently above me. I found myself trying to not eat, going on week-long liquid diets, taking diet pills like Dexatrim and even Ex Lax. They worked short term and then it wasn't enough. I needed it to work faster, have better results. Unknowingly I found myself face to face with what I called a mild cycle of anorexia. Before long I became unhappy with my body. With the "it's not enough" mentality, I found myself forming a secret life. I was throwing up behind everyone's back, feeling guilty and ashamed, but not quitting because I thought I wasn't doing it enough to hurt anyone. I had often wished the weight would drop, so it would be my last time, but Lady Luck never dealt her cards that way for me.

My sophomore year was the worst. I denied my problems and let them take over. My friends stuck by me but hated how I changed. They gave me nicknames that I'd simply laugh off and not face. I started to realize the extent of my obsession when my best friend confessed how worried she was. She said she thought I might die, and if I did, she would feel guilty for never telling anyone. I had never known how much I had put not only myself through, but the people I cared about as well. She got me in a group at school. I felt weird, like I was exposed; it wasn't a secret. I still allowed it to be the monkey on my back, to let it control me. My life revolved around the being-skinny concept.

Why did I do it? Why do I still have urges? Because I didn't want to be judged badly, because I didn't want to be the joke, because even though it's wrong, I'd rather be judged for size four rather than shunned for my old size eleven. It's hard to set apart and differentiate between realistic and unrealistic goals. It's a struggle. It's an addiction that enticed me, because I feel everyone's waiting for me to change and I don't want to disappoint them.

Society is at fault for relaying the wrong perception: that only the thin is OK. I also blame myself, for allowing it to overpower me and spur conformity in me, for confusing myself out of everything I've worked for: pride, self worth, and individualism.

I'm not completely over this. I don't think I ever will be. It will take a lifetime to deal with my experience and not allow myself to be dragged in again. But as long as society continues these attitudes and impressions, I will try my best to be the one who says, "Enough." I will speak for those who are falling deeper into the game and often feel futile because the stakes are placed too high. I have to. If I don't, everything associated with the problem will have won. I can't let that happen, to me, or to the thousands of girls who are too silent and ashamed. I just cannot allow them to win.

MY INCREDIBLE JOURNEY

Kristin Schmitz

My name is Kristin Schmitz. My problem started when I was in fourth grade. I was overweight. Fourth grade was the time when everyone in class started looking at others with criticism. With five years of my life behind me, I look back and feel as if I was cheated out of my happiness.

When I was younger I attended a private Catholic school, from kindergarten through sixth grade. There was an average of twenty five students in a grade, and approximately one hundred-fifty kids in the whole school. Every kid knew who everyone else was, which made it even harder for me, because I not only got picked on by the kids in my grade, but everyone else that was older than me too. Beginning in the fourth grade, everyone teased me and it only got worse as I became older. I was told to use Slim Fast, and that I should go run off all my fat. These are just a few of the things that I would hear every day. After two years of this torment my self-confidence and self-esteem decreased faster than one can only imagine.

The summer between my fourth- and fifth-grade year I made a promise to myself that I would lose weight. My goal wasn't achieved that summer; it truly became worse. My fifth-grade year was one big joke. As my classmates became older, they also became meaner. I became so angry with them, it was all I could do to keep myself from crying and screaming at everyone. Of course I didn't intend to tell them all off, because I wasn't able to defend myself due to the lack of self-esteem. I attended a Catholic school, and they did not allow being mean, yelling, and swearing. The summer came, I set the same goal and nothing happened. Sixth grade was only worse, but my goal wasn't achieved then either.

Seventh grade finally came and I was going to attend the public school, because I had enough of that living hell. I left behind all my so-called "friends," goals, and memories from that school. I was terrified. I knew only the fifteen other girls that I had played softball and basketball with. Going to school was something some kids looked forward to, because seventh grade was in the high school, so we would all be with the big kids. But for me not only would there be one hundred kids to tease me in my grade, there would be five hundred kids in the whole school. Much to my surprise, that year was the best year I had in three years. No one teased me, I had many real friends, and I had much fun. The only thing that set me apart from others was that I still had low self-esteem and a weight problem. The summer before my eighth-grade year, I tried desperately to lose weight. All I ever wanted was to have an admirable figure, because it seemed that was all that was surrounding me. I thought being thin was expected of people. Nothing happened that summer.

Eighth grade came and I was beginning to enjoy the public school immensely. People were so polite it was almost unbelievable. Surrounding me my whole life had been mean, crabby people. I began to look at things with a better perspective. I was still very self-conscious and unsure of others. I realized that a great body wasn't everything, but that was still what I wanted. The summer came, and I set the same goal I had all the other years. Nothing happened. I didn't understand why, but it didn't bother me as much as it had in the past. I didn't gain weight, but I wasn't losing weight either.

My ninth-grade year was great, I was almost unstoppable. I realized that people at my school didn't judge me on my appearance, so I decide to join activities that would take up more of my time and raise my self-esteem and self-confidence. I had been in the musical the year before so I joined again. Some of my other activities included Speech, Mock Trial, Solo and Ensemble, and Track. The most important activity I was in was Cheerleading. It helped me get out and show my spirit, but most of all it helped build my confidence up. When summer came I decided it was time for a change, but I had no idea what kind. I was becoming a different person who wanted a physical change. The only problem was I had no idea how to do it!

Actually, I was afraid. Afraid that nothing would happen, just like before. Finally, I realized that it wasn't that important to me, and I would take whatever happened. Well, I was so busy that I didn't have much time to worry about it. I had a job, and one day I was eating lunch with a woman who began talking about how people really need to watch their intake of fats unless they want to risk dying from a heart attack, and better yet, one can also lose weight. That was my ticket out, and it didn't sound too difficult. Reality struck me when I came home to a house full of junk food. I realized that it wasn't going to be as easy as it sounded. I limited myself to certain foods and became a label reader. I decided that I had liked running in track so I decided to start running for exercise. I began to feel great and look a lot better. I changed that summer: from sizes nine and eleven to five and seven.

Finally it came time for me to face friends I hadn't seen since the last day of ninth grade. I went back to school as a new person, and everyone noticed. People came up to me and told me that I looked great, besides that I felt great! I also saw some of my classmates from my old school and they felt terrible for all the mean things that they said and did when they saw how I had changed. For the first time I felt as though I achieved a goal—a goal that I thought I could never reach but only dream of. My classmates came to me for advice on how to lose weight or tone their body. I was so happy, and it felt great to be on the other side for a change.

My sophomore year of high school is almost over, and I have managed to keep off the weight I lost. I have been on my wonderful diet for nearly nine months without totally losing my cool. This has been by far the most difficult thing that I have ever accomplished. I am very proud of my hard work, and my family and friends are proud of me as well.

GETTING STARTED

Anonymous

While filling the shoes of a center may be the most exciting position on the court, playing guard is the toughest place to be by far while playing a game—a game of basketball that is. Being the shortest seventh-grade player on the street is even tougher. My height is always keeping me from getting the orange thing in the basket.

The one person who taught me how to play a good game is my brother. Simply the best on the street—don't bet against him. Believe it or not, I'm getting better with his help. I'm still the worst player on the court whenever I'm in there. In fact, you'd be better leaving me on the bench if I played on your team.

I don't shoot well enough to be a shooter. I don't score enough to be a scorer. I don't rebound enough to be a banger. Come to think of it, I don't pass the ball that well, and I'm not much on defense. So is this the year I get my act together? Probably not.

So why do I like playing games that are usually for tall people? Well, because I like it. And because it makes me feel tall, even though there can be a 6'6" giant standing above me. Since I'm only 4'10", most people are at least a couple inches taller than I am. And since I'm so enthusiastic, they let me play.

There's two parts to this problem. The first part is I'm short. I know it doesn't seem tough to be a runt, but at times, you can feel as big as a peanut and twice as dumb.

The second part is the fact I'm nowhere close to being the next Larry Johnson, but maybe with luck I can be the next Muggsy Bogues. And although both of these problems put together isn't anything like racism, abuse, or being paralyzed, it can be frustrating.

There is pressure you face every day in this world.

ILLNESS AND DISABILITY

t for the country's
nixed. While there
rvices to assit street
en table, her sitting,
nock, the interrogation began
me control over his future
behavior set in a
their some I
much here in
when he hit me. I'd
and he the table
lying in the hammock, th

ILLNESS AND DISABILITY

Four of the five essays in this section deal with the writer's own disability or illness. The fifth essay is about the disability of a family member and its effects on the author.

Isaac Toso writes about how his life changes when he is operated on for a brain tumor. He tells us about the operation itself and his struggles afterward to learn to walk, talk, and read all over again. All the time he relies on his religion to get him through. It is a story of faith, support, and strength.

Amber Junker has spina bifida and is in a wheelchair. We learn what this means in very specific ways. She says that now she has gotten used to her disability and describes how she worries about peer pressure and sibling relationships, just like any other young person.

Suzanne Colby's essay is the shortest in the book. Its length relates to her learning disability. She says that reading, writing, and understanding are difficult for her. And in the end, she says, "I wouldn't change anything about myself."

Daisy has a similar disability. She calls her story "My Problem." In the original copy of the essay the word *Problem* was spelled with the letters going backward to illustrate what life is like when one sees things in reverse. Because she does not "look different" from other kids, Daisy is not diagnosed early and has to struggle on her own for quite awhile before she gets any help. These two essays give us such a clear picture of what life with a disability is like and how much it takes to overcome it.

In a beautifully written essay, Michelle Humphrey takes us through the discovery of her diabetes, her instruction in insulin injection, and the changes that have happened in her life because of this illness. She has had counseling and support and we are left finishing this narrative with great hope for Michelle.

While it does not deal with his own illness, Mathew Gifford's essay, "The Perfect Morning" is included in this section because it shows the profound effect his mother's multiple sclerosis has had on the his family. He opens his story with the words: "The only memory that I have of my mother being healthy is brief but very vivid." We go on to experience the subsequent deterioration of his mother. He is honest about his feelings, his sadness, his yearning for a healthy mother again. This is told with compassion and without self-pity and says as much about Matthew's courage as it does about his mother's struggle.

HE WILL RAISE YOU UP

Isaac Toso

My name is Isaac Toso. The name, Isaac, means "laughter." I like my name because I like to laugh. My mother likes the name because she says it reminds her of when Abraham's wife, Sarah, heard that she was going to have a baby at the age of ninety, she laughed. But God said, "Is anything too hard for the Lord?" Allow me to tell my story of how the Lord God has shown me that nothing is too difficult for Him.

In February of 1991 I went over to the Mayo Clinic to have a neurological exam because of a tremor in my left hand. I had to go through a series of tests and examinations to find out what was wrong. The doctor discovered pressure behind my eyes. To find out what was causing it, he ordered a CAT scan of my head. This all happened on a Thursday afternoon, and when all of the tests were completed I was exhausted. We got some rather shocking news: There was a brain tumor the size of a softball in my brain. An astrocytoma is a type of cancer that grows slowly over a long period of time, so we do not know when it started growing. Because of where it was located at the brain stem and because of its size, an emergency surgery was scheduled.

That weekend was the most frightening time of my life. Dr. Kelly, my surgeon, told us that I needed surgery in order to stay alive, but I was afraid that I might die. I am told that the Bible verse that comforted me when I was afraid was: "If we live, we live to the Lord, and if we die, we die to the Lord; so then, whether we live or whether we die, we are the Lord's" (Romans 14:8).

The surgery lasted for sixteen hours, in which the famous and excellent brain surgeon, Dr. Kelly, operated on my brain to remove the tumor.

Doing this type of surgery is a very complicated job, and it is very stressful. I am very thankful that I had such an excellent brain surgeon operating on me. Many people around the world were praying for me. Every couple of hours a nurse was sent into the waiting room to inform my family and friends about how the operation was progressing. Close to midnight my family was told that the surgery was done. I had survived, but they did not know what the outcome would be.

After being in a coma for a week, I was moved from intensive care to the pediatric unit. For the next three weeks, I was wheeled to physical, speech, and occupational therapy twice a day. I needed to relearn how to walk, use my hands, and talk again.

I was brought home one month after surgery. I continued an extensive program of physical and occupational therapy to help my muscles to recover and help my mind to learn how to do what it needed to do again. I remember being so frustrated sometimes because an activity like walking was a real challenge for me to do in my condition. After I learned to walk, my mom and dad bought me a bicycle helmet with money from gifts, and then they secretly taught me to ride a bike again. (The doctor would have frowned on my bike riding because I might have fallen and reinjured myself.)

When school started in September I could walk the nine blocks to school on my own. I needed the help of a classroom aide, a person to accompany me, because I couldn't remember where to go or what to do next.

It has been five years since then. I study a lot at home to help me remember the information I am taught at school. Sometimes I get frustrated because even though I do a lot of studying I still can't remember all of the information I need to. I was nervous before ninth grade started, since I would have to adjust to a new school building. For me, this means a longer time to learn how to get from one place to the next. Mrs. Hoff, an instructional aide, has been an excellent guide to help me remember how to get from one class to the next during each class period. Another helpful thing she does is to find out when tests are going to be so I can prepare for them. She helps me review my subjects during study hall every day. All this shows me that God really cares for me.

In my free time I enjoy playing violin and going to the YMCA to swim, lift weights, and run on the track. I also enjoy being with my friends and fooling around with them. A song that was sung at my Grandpa's funeral that I really like is called "On Eagle's Wings" by Michael Jonas. These words are based on Psalm 91: "You who dwell in the shelter of the Lord, who abide in His shadow for life, say to the Lord, 'My refuge in whom I trust.' And He will raise you up on eagle's wings, bear you on the breath of dawn, make you to shine like the sun, and hold you in the palm of His hand."

That song means a lot to me because that is exactly what the Lord has done for me after the operation.

LIFE WITH A DISABILITY

Amber Junker

I have a disability called spina bifida, which has prevented me from being able to walk; so I use a wheelchair to get me around. Being in a wheelchair isn't easy because I have a lot of things to deal with. It is not easy for me to go to a lot of places because they aren't handicapped-accessible, even though they may say they are. Some examples of places like this are restrooms in buildings such as hotels and restaurants; also state park hiking trails, showers, and restrooms. Having this disability has given me lots more than this to deal with. I have to deal with people as well. Some of them are more rude and inconsiderate to me than they would be to an able-bodied person, just because I'm handicapped. People think that just because I can't use my legs I can't use the rest of my body and they think I can't do as much as I can. I can do a lot—just not as well as others. That is one way I differ from others.

I can't do any sports that require using legs since I can't walk. That does not mean I can't enjoy sports. Aside from being disabled and in a wheelchair, I have a few of the same problems other teens my age have. Problems such as death and peer pressure. Other problems I don't have but I know are problems are violence, AIDS, drugs and alcohol, and gangs.

Hopefully I won't have any of these problems in the future. Why death is a problem to me is because my dad died when I was fourteen years old. Peer pressure comes along when I am with friends. I tend to pick on my little brother more often when my friends are around. I don't really mind my disability anymore. I have gotten used to it over the years. But I think people should get to know me better. Then they would be nicer because they would realize I'm really not a bad person.

While it has not been easy to deal with my disability, luckily I have some really terrific friends. I don't know what I would do without them. They have been a big help. I think it helps that I have a positive attitude about myself, and also, it helps that I am really so independent.

WHAT IT TAKES

Suzanne Colby

My name is Suzanne Colby and the challenges I am trying to overcome are my disabilities. I have a learning disability and hearing loss. I also take growth hormones to help me grow. Twice a day I also take Ritalin to help me concentrate at school.

Some things that are difficult for me are reading, writing, and understanding. I get teased by other kids about how I walk and about liking Barney, and I feel like it's hard to make friends.

I get a lot of help at school to overcome my challenges. I have a teacher for deafness/hard of hearing who helps me with my school work. I also work with the learning disabilities teacher on math. I work with the speech clinician to improve my speech. The school counselor helps me talk about how I feel when kids tease me. My best friend takes notes for me in class. My teachers help me when I don't understand in class.

It is a challenge to be a person with special needs, but I wouldn't change anything about myself.

MY PROBLEM
Daisy

I guess I have what most people would call a perfect life. I have a lot of acquaintances, some friends, and a few best friends. I get straight-A's most of the time. I am very athletic and do sports year round. There's only one little snag in this fairy tale of a life. I have dyslexia, which is a disorder where I see letters and numbers backward. It's like if a person with regular vision took a sentence that they wrote on a piece of paper and looked at it in the mirror, all the letters would be flipped.

I guess I was born with it because when I started writing, around six or seven years old, I had trouble with my p's, q's, d's, and b's. I always wrote them backwards and got them all mixed up. I can still see my first-grade teacher towering over me and telling me to write them over until I got it right. When I started writing I really had to concentrate. While the other second- and third-graders played at recess, I would sit down with my handwriting book and figure out how each letter was written in the "right way," the opposite of mine.

I knew my letters were wrong because all the kids in my class used to think it was cool that I could write backwards without a mirror. That was devastating. From that point on I was determined to be normal, or at least write normal.

I was always a little behind. When the teacher would give an assignment I always had it done last. I dreaded reading time because we had fifteen minutes to read a short story, but it always took me double the time because I had to first turn the letters around in my head, and then turn the words around to make sense.

My mom tells me now that the school system failed in not noticing that I was having trouble, but since I was getting good grades I don't think they were too concerned. I was never teased about it because I didn't look any different from the other kids and they didn't know anything about my problem.

When I was eleven or twelve I was watching a movie about an old man who never learned to read because he had dyslexia. At that time I had no idea what that was but as I watched the movie I saw that the man had the same problem that I do. So I told my parents that I thought I had dyslexia, too. My parents didn't believe me at first; they thought I was just trying to get attention. But then I told them that I would write down the letters exactly how I saw them, I did it for them and then they believed me.

My mom talked to the social workers at my school and they gave me some tests. According to the tests I had the knowledge of a college student; on one of the new tests I was the first person to get it right. All the special education people called me "Einstein Jr." for the rest of my sixth-grade year.

I am in eighth grade now and have survived two years of middle school with my problem. As you can see, I am now a fairly good writer and I can write pretty fast. In classes I can take notes just as fast as the next person and now I am at normal reading level.

Some days I don't even think about it, but sometimes I hit one of my limits and am bounced back into place. I'm still waiting to be just as famous as Einstein.

ABNORMAL

Michelle Humphrey

My initial reaction was to blame my mother. She's the woman that gave birth to me—and I love her with all my heart, but for some reason, I still put the blame on her. (Besides, it had to go somewhere.)

"I'm never going to be normal again," I thought to myself as my mother drove me to St. Marys Hospital. I was 14 years old and all of a sudden, my world was turning inside out. I was a typical freshman student—good grades, good friends, good health—or so I thought. For the few weeks prior to that fateful day, I had been feeling different. Not sick, just different. I had been drinking anything in sight and using the bathroom more frequently. One morning, I drank a gallon of juice before heading off to school. At night, I would be getting up anywhere from three to six times to use the bathroom. Simple walks up small inclines would leave me breathless and shaking. Seven pounds thinner, I began to wonder, "What's happening with me?"

I remember the day so vividly—February 13, 1991—the day before Valentine's Day. My friends and I sat excitedly at our usual back-corner lunch table. I looked up from the table, anticipating the arrival of the rest of my friends; instead, I saw the assistant principal of John Adams Jr. High approaching me.

"I just got off the phone with your mother. She's coming to pick you up now, and she wants you to wait outside, in front of the building."

"Why?" I inquired. My mother never picked me up early from school.

"Just go get your things. You've already been excused from your afternoon classes." And with that, he walked away.

After what seemed like hours of waiting in the cold, winter afternoon, my mother finally arrived. I sat in mother's 1990 Ford comfortably, letting the heat absorb into my numb body.

Unsure of what lay ahead of me and confused as to why she had picked me up early from school and was driving us to the hospital, I asked, "What's up?"

I could tell something big was bothering her and I had a feeling that after she told me, it would bother me too. She hesitated a moment, then trying to be brave, she ventured into what would be known as the beginning of the rest of my life. "Well, your doctor called me this morning . . . ."

I thought back to my annual check-up the week before. Nothing was unusual about it—I had only mentioned that I was drinking and using the bathroom more frequently. I figured I was having bladder problems and now we were going to take care of it.

". . . And she thinks you're a diabetic."

"What?" I asked as my voice started to tremble. I stared blankly out the car window, unsure if I had heard her correctly. The only thing I knew about diabetes was that those "uncool" and "unsociable" people had to take multiple shots daily. I figured no guy would ever want to go out with me after he found out I was a diabetic. I felt a lump swelling in my throat and I threw my hands to my face as the raindrops started sliding from my eyes. "I don't want to be a diabetic," I sobbed.

"I know honey. If I could take your place, I would." Concern showed in my mother's voice, but it wasn't good enough. I didn't want concern, I wanted to be normal.

Slowly, I turned my face towards her and, to my surprise, tears had swollen her eyes too.

"I don't understand how or why?" I managed to get out through muffled cries.

"I've thought about it, and I don't understand either. My grandmother was a diabetic but she had adult diabetes. The doctor told me that diabetes can skip some generations."

Anger. That's all I could feel at the time. "There's no way you can take my place. I'm the one who has to live with this—not you. And it's your fault—you and your grandmother's. You're the one that should have this —not me!" I thought to myself with hopeless anger.

Up in my boring, white, disinfected walls of my hospital room, new faces swarmed around me—people with starch white lab coats on, people with thermometers sticking out of their pockets, people with stethoscopes around their necks—but most of all, people that I wanted to leave me alone.

"How are you doing today?" Someone in a white coat asked, walking into my room. I assumed he would be my doctor.

"How the hell do you think I'm doing?" I thought to myself. "You people just told me I'm a diabetic. That I'm going to have to take two shots of insulin a day, prick my fingers at least four times a day, watch every morsel of food I put into my mouth, check my urine anytime my blood sugars are over 240 to see if ketones are spilling, and deal with insulin reactions on a day-to-day basis. Mockingly, I answered, "Fine."

"Everything will work out for you. Millions of people are diabetics and learn to control it on a day-to-day basis. Mikhail Gorbachev is a diabetic."

"Well hip-hip-hooray for him," I thought. "I'm not Mikhail Gorbachev, I'm Michelle Humphrey, and I'm the one who has to deal and live with this "thing" for the rest of life."

The doctor finally left me alone, and I ran to my mom for comfort. A lump started swelling in my throat again, and I let the tears flow. It was reassuring to hold my mom and know that she was right by my side; together, we held each other and cried.

After a few days in the hospital, it was finally time to give myself a shot on my own. The nurse and my mom stood over me like guardian angels, making sure everything was going all right. I drew up my insulin and was holding the needle in my hand. "You can do it Michelle—you have to in order to live," a voice inside me kept repeating. Suddenly, the room seemed like it was caving in on me and I knew it was time—there was no more stalling. With my hand shaking, I jabbed the sharp point into my left thigh and released the insulin from the needle, into my system. Some blood started oozing out after I pulled the needle out.

"That's all right the nurse told me comforting. A little blood comes out from time to time."

I did it! I gave myself my first shot! Relief filled my body and I was able to relax again—that is until, the next morning when I would have to do it all over again.

During my stay at the hospital, I was introduced to new learning techniques I would have to incorporate in my daily lifestyle. One class taught me how to use my blood sugar machine correctly. Normal range for blood sugars are between 70-120 and I was to try and stay as close as possible to those numbers. Anything lower than 70, I would have a reaction and would have to get some sugar in my system immediately. Anything too high, I would have to take more insulin the next time I was to give myself a shot. The importance of proper blood sugar control became very apparent to me after I landed in the hospital a year later. I was almost in a diabetic coma due to improper blood sugar management.

Another class taught me how to exchange my foods correctly. For example, a half of a banana or small apple equal one fruit exchange. Two ounces of meat equal one meat exchange. No candy or pies—anything good—were incorporated into my new "diet" for life. Sometimes, when I had an insulin reaction, I would use it as an excuse to pig out on candy.

One week and one day later I was released from the hospital. At home, only little things reminded me of my new life. I cleared away a spot in one of my drawers, to keep my machine and insulin in. My mother had bought a medic alert bracelet identifying that I am insulin dependent. I told her

I would never wear it and to this day, I still haven't put it on once. She also bought a diabetic recipe book and a weight machine, so I could measure out all my food.

My family kept telling me this was a good thing that happened—now we could all become healthier. But I couldn't understand how this could be a good thing. How could taking shots daily be good?

Looking back now, I can't say that I blame my mother directly—or anyone else for that matter. Diabetes is just something unfortunate that happens to individuals.

It has taken me three years and professional counseling to finally let go of all the pain and confusion I once had felt. But, learning how to cope and manage my diabetes has made me realize that diabetics can lead a normal, happy life.

THE PERFECT MORNING

Mathew Gifford

The only memory that I have of my mother being healthy is brief, but very vivid.

It comes as if it were a scene in a long forgotten movie. She was sitting in the driver 's seat of our odd, dark blue, 1978 station wagon, driving me to preschool. Just sitting there . . . riding. With both hands curling around the steering wheel, she turned her beautiful sunlit face to me and smiled—a mother's smile that could instantly dash away any fears and warm the heart. That single smile will always take me back to when times were perfect, when times were as they should be now. During this time I had no worries or cares in the world; during this time my mother did not have multiple sclerosis.

"Stop the car! You're going to hit something! Please stop!"

The car swerved back to the right, out of the opposite lane, and into our own. I searched for and grabbed the door handle to counter the force and alleviate the tremendous shock that swept over me. These instant emotions of sheer horror were new to my ten-year-old self. She cranked the wheel to the right again, and at the same time slammed on the brakes. The car slid on the loose gravel on the shoulder of the road and ground to a halt. My mother and I just sat there silently, her hand white from the pressure, still firmly locked onto the wheel. The engine was no longer running and the smell of burned tire pervaded the interior of the car. I looked down and stared at the Wilson baseball mitt I had used in that day's fourth-grade game.

After what seemed like hours I finally asked her, "What's wrong, Mom?" As I watched her face for any sign of response or movement, I noticed her eyes appear to well up with tears.

"I don t know," she said. "Oh God I don t know."

At that moment I knew, only one year after she had been diagnosed with multiple sclerosis, that my mother would never be the same again. Oh sure, our family had noted that the disease had weakened her a little during the past year; but this incident was more of a confirmation that it really existed. With that one tear it was evident my mother's defenses had failed and the disease succeeded in its assault of her life, our lives. A page had slowly turned to a new chapter in my mother's life, and she was never the same again.

My sister, brother, and I walked apprehensively down the halls of St. Joseph's hospital. The usual stagnant, sterile smell of the air was present. The halls were dark and were uncannily silent except for a few scattered, hushed conversations by the nurses. The intensive care unit was laid out in circular fashion, with the rooms around the perimeter and the main nurse's desk positioned in the center.

We peered into the first room and saw that it was occupied by an elderly man laying on his side sleeping. The next room had another elderly man, supported by his walker, staring out of the window at the rear of the room. As we came up to the adjacent room I looked in and saw a small, frail woman laying in bed and her husband, presumably, hunched over her with his back to us. My glance shifted from the room to the next ahead when I felt a hand tighten around my arm.

"Wait, Matthew. Mom and Dad are in here," my sister said.

"What?!" I angrily snapped back at her. I had not spoken all day and the emotions of anger, fear, and fatigue pent up inside me exploded in my response.

She looked solemnly at me and then pointed to the room I had just passed. A tingling sensation and a wave of sheer terror rushed through my body as my fears were quickly confirmed.

My body was numb as I followed her into the room. When I entered. I saw my brother on the other side of the bed, his cheeks moist with tears shimmering from the light above.

My father turned around slowly and quietly said, "Hello." He looked exhausted. His face was pale, his eyes glassy and sagging. The wrinkles in his ever-aging face seemed exaggerated, a testament to his fatigue. He had gone without sleep for almost thirty hours.

The mother that had left the airport for a summer vacation in the Netherlands only one week before was totally different from the woman that lay before me now. When the "attack" happened, my father had to rush to get her back to the United States. She had been so energetic in anticipation of this trip. It was not often that she got the chance to leave the house, let alone travel. Before the trip I could see in her smiles of anticipation and joy—a hint of how she looked as we drove to preschool that memorable morning. She had been born again, with a revitalized zest for life.

Now she looked so fragile, so hollow. Her face was gaunt and weary with exhaustion. She struggled to keep her eyes open. Her head turned to me as she extended out a trembling hand. I took it and could feel how tired she was. In a slurred, broken voice she whispered. "Could have been worse, honey."

"Yeah Mom, I know."

Now confined to a wheelchair, my mother has become a very withdrawn and bitter person, mostly due to loneliness. Many seem to have forgotten about her because of this disease. Some of her friends, however, have stuck with her and keep in contact either with visits, letters, or phone calls.

I try to spend as much time as possible with my mother. However, at times I think of when she will be gone and how guilty I might feel for all the times I could have sat down and talked with her, or how frustrated and angry I sometimes felt when she asked me to help her with something. I do not mind the added responsibilities like cooking and cleaning. Especially now, since I am the only child still at home I find that a large amount of my free-time is spent working around the house and running errands.

The worst part of this disease is how gradual and constant it is. It wears away at the sufferer, slowly sapping the vitality out of them. Over the years, I have seen what it has done to my mother both mentally and physically. I wonder if it will ever end.

I often find myself thinking back to that innocent, carefree morning as my mother and I drove to preschool. This image will forever be bolted into my memory, never to be forgotten. It was so perfect. All I want is to have back the mother I never had.

DEPRESSION

for the country's
ixed. While there
rvices to assit street
n table, her sitting,
ock, the interrogation began
ne control over his future
~~ioral~~ ~~behavior~~ ~~learned~~ set in a
~~ptured~~
~~their arms~~
~~always so much here~~ in
~~themselves~~
hen he hit me. I'd
~~upstair and he would hit~~ ~~kitchen table~~
lying in the hammock, th

DEPRESSION

Considering the problems that young people face today, we should not be surprised that one of the biggest essay categories is on depression.

Kaitlin Joy Mclachlan opens her essay with a poem entitled; "Death": "One more day/one more hour/one more minute, I cannot take." We accompany her on her journey into that darkness that is true depression. It is harrowing. We realize at the end that after a suicide attempt and time in an institution, she is beginning to live in the present.

Spencer Foxworth writes with equal beauty, in a more philosophical way, about coming to terms with his own depression. He opens with "Evening now, and dark." We sit with him during a long night of introspection. He has learned to accept himself, as well as the problems in society and has found a way to live with it all. In evocative language, Spencer takes us deeply inside his heart.

Midway through her story, Maura says: "There I was, afraid and alone. I was alone because I shut everyone out. I had no friends. Nothing could get inside of me because I thought everything would hurt me." She has come out of this now and we feel her relief.

"And what a life I had. I practically lived inside my bedroom, with my door always locked and music as my only companion," says Elizabeth Neil in her essay entitled "Black Days Gone Gray." We see that she kept up outward appearances so that no one guessed how seriously she was depressed. We go inside her mind on her worst days. And finally, we come out of this depression with her.

In the last essay in this group, Matthew Byrne takes us into that dark place with him, too. And then he takes us up and out of it. Finally, at the end, he thanks his friends for their support. In this essay we learn exactly what it feels like to be sad all the time, how alone such people become, and how lost they feel. In this story, as in the others, we are made aware of the seriousness of such feelings, of how vulnerable and fragile our young people are, even when they may appear to be fine.

We complete this section with some new resolve to make certain that our sons and daughters, our students, friends and relatives know they have a place to go when things get so lonely and so full of darkness.

A NEW DAY WILL DAWN

Kaitlin Joy Mclachlan

DEATH

One more day
One more hour
One more minute
I can not take
It hurts,
It hurts so bad
And so very deep
My body shakes
And the tears come
They seep from my eyes
Like a powerful rainstorm
No control
No longer
Death..

And so began my journey of self-discovery. For the first time in my life I let myself realize that I wasn't perfect. That I wasn't my daddy's little baby girl. That I wasn't like everyone else. I had always felt that I was different from all the other kids, yet I never knew why. It seems that the older I got, the more I seemed to stray from the norm. Of course being the "perfect" little girl I was, no one would ever suspect that there was something wrong. But I knew in my heart that there was something very wrong with the way I was.

By the time I entered the sixth grade I had given up wondering and had taken up hiding. I no longer wondered why I felt so very depressed and angry all the time, because I was determined to hide from those feelings. I was determined to hide from the emotions that burned inside of me. I was determined to hide from any differences that set me apart from the beautiful, happy girls that were in my class. I was determined to hide myself. Hiding from my illness didn't really work as well as I had planned. Oh sure, during the day I seemed happy to everyone else, but one can only hide from oneself for so long. I soon found myself being shaken awake at night by horrid nightmares and uncontrollable crying fits. I hated myself to my very core, and the more I tried to deny who I really was, the more I seemed to suffer.

My frightful nights soon started to overtake my days. I dreaded going to school more than anything, I hated the people who I tried so hard to be like: all those beautiful popular girls who thought they could tell me what to do, who thought they were so much better than I was. Because I thought they were better than I was, I also figured I should do what they told me to do.

Of course I can't forget the boys. Those boys who were even more beautiful than the girls, and they knew it. Those lovely boys who let me tag along, who let me fall in love with them and later would shatter my dreams. All those beautiful, perfect, people who waited for me at school. All those beautiful, perfect people who were so very different from me.

My mornings turned into a battle field between my father and me. Every morning I refused to go to school, usually far too sick with a mysterious illness to drag myself into the world of perfect sixth-graders who awaited me. My father, being the rigid and structured man he was, would all but drag me out of bed to get me to go to school. I knew it killed him to see me defy him; I knew he wanted nothing more than for me to go to school, but I couldn't. I also knew that meant that I could no longer be his perfect little girl. Somewhere along the line, I decided that my relationship with my father was going to have to be sacrificed, for the sake of my life. You see all this time my nights had been getting much worse.

All the anger that I had suppressed all day was beginning to come out. Yet no matter what, it was always toward me. I could always find a way to blame myself. I would cut the soles of my feet to shreds, so as every step I took would cause me great pain. I figured I deserved the pain, since the way I was happened to be so different from what God meant for me to be, so unlike the child anyone would ever want. I began to collect other devices to physically harm myself, maybe to eventually kill myself.

The year slowly passed, and somehow I was able to make it through. My final report card looked something like this: "Total days absent—86." Additional comments: "Very unmotivated. Absence affects work. Gone too often. Must work harder, etc." I really let my parents down and I'm well aware of it, but at the time I didn't think there was anything that I could do.

My summer came and my summer went. I think summers have always been easier on me. All I had to do was sleep, eat, and remember to breathe. Those are some pretty low stress requirements. Yet in just a few months I found a way to stress myself out—Jr. High.

I started seventh grade, and, at first, things seemed to go great. I was popular enough to satisfy my ego, I made it to school almost every day, and for some strange reason those beautiful boys stood up and acknowledged me. The first of that year is when I did my best hiding ever. For once in my life I had all those things I thought brought true happiness to anyone who could obtain them. Yet I still wasn't happy. Well I'll be damned if I'm going to risk all this due to these stupid emotions, I thought, so I continued trying to be a beautiful, happy, perfect, young girl. In other words, I tried to be everything I wasn't.

There wasn't an exact day or week—or even month for that matter—that my depression really started to set in. I think it was something that was destined to happen. I slowly sank farther and farther in a black world. A world filled with shattered dreams, tears, and the fear that I may never escape. My "wonderful" new-found popularity, and my "wonderful" new friends started to slip away as I became "that weird girl who wears black and sits by herself." By that time I was so far gone that I really didn't care. I noticed something very important then, though. I noticed that those "nerdy girls" that I had kind of become friends with stayed next to me and made me smile. I noticed that even though all the "hockey players" may want to sleep with me, it was the "headbanging druggie" who always stayed by me to make sure I never felt lonely. I realized that all those names I had thrown around in my pursuit of popularity really didn't mean anything, that it was the people who I thought were the least important turned out to be much more important than any of those immaculate popular bitches.

I started to go out with that "headbanging druggie." Turns out he didn't listen to headbanging music at all and that he had been trying to quit doing drugs and gave them up for me. He had no idea what he had just gotten himself into. No matter how great my life was, my depression worsened and worsened. I turned to him constantly, for he was the first person I had ever met who I felt I could talk to. I first admitted to him that I often felt depressed for no reason, and that first time I admitted it to him was also the first time I had really admitted it to myself. I didn't realize it then, but like with any problem the first step you have to take to recovery is one of admitting your illness.

I began to slowly be able to write and draw about the feelings that controlled the way my life had been lived for so long. It soon became my only refuge from my worsening depression. My nights got to be much worse than they had been the year before, my sleep was limited to random minutes, and even then the nightmares I experienced would shake me awake. I tried to stop talking to people very much; I felt I would only bother them with my problems. So I was back again with all of my feelings bottled up inside of me, and I was refusing to ask for help from anyone.

I wrote the poem you read in the beginning of my tale the night before I first attempted to commit suicide. That night I lay awake and cried for hours straight, like all the other nights that I had experienced the past few months. I decided that I couldn't go on like that any longer. First I tried to make amends with God, fearing that I would end up in Hell. Then I crept downstairs to slip two bottles of extra-strength aspirin from the medicine cabinet in to my school bag. I felt it very important not to die, or at least not kill myself, in my parents' home. They had lived there for thirty years and had built half of it themselves. I knew if I did die, my death would be hard enough for them to deal with, without the memories of finding my body lurking over this house. So in a morning after no sleep whatsoever, I put on my very favorite outfit and tried to make myself look as nice as possible. I remember standing at my bus stop and thinking that it was a good day to die. And even though I would die, so would all the pain that I had felt for so very long. After this point my memory begins to blur. I remember swallowing all two hundred-fifty pills in the bathroom on the bottom floor of my school. I remember my boyfriend having to practically carry me in to the nurses' office, and I remember his tears that fell on to my body. I can still remember the look on my mother's face as she watched them put me on to a stretcher and hoist me in to the ambulance.

This is where I pretty much passed out. But I remember feeling my stomach retch as the doctor pumped it. I woke up to my body having spasms due to all the drugs that were passing through my veins. An hour later they sent me home, no questions asked, no precautions taken. So they probably shouldn't have been surprised when I showed up a month later. Only this time I was in another unit.

I entered a place called Willow Street just as they were winding down for the day. I had never been so frightened in my life. I had been told that afternoon that I had to be placed in a hospital for "troubled" teens. I guess my psychiatrist didn't think quitting school and laying in bed crying for a week was a very good sign, I can't imagine why not. So doctor's orders— put Kaitlin in a loony bin. At least that's all I really got out of it at first.

My days at Willow Street were some of the worst, best and most interesting days that I've ever experienced. I met great people and had many good laughs and a few good cries. That's where I found a lot of other people who were suffering from the same feelings and fears that I had kept inside. I also started to take medication for my depression while I was in there, a common cure for clinical and manic depression. I realized I was not alone and that people can not only live their lives but succeed in their lives. These incredible people who suffer from the same disease that I had picked up the shattered pieces of their lives and were happy. They became my inspiration. I wanted to be happy. I wanted to show kids like me who were ready to give up that they can make it through.

After a month and a half in the hospital, I was sent home. I know I learned more in that hospital than I could have ever learned in school, and that those lessons are far more important. I learned that no matter what, I've got to come first in my life. I took that to heart and spent the next year of my life trying to discover the happy child I once was before depression had taken over.

I know the years I lost to depression are years that I will never get back. But more importantly, I know God gives me a new day every morning— a day to do all those things I lost, a day to pick flowers and lay in the grass, a day to giggle in class with my best friend, a day that is mine and mine only. There are millions of days that lay ahead of me and a future as bright as I want to make it. I thank God that I didn't die that day because I realized that my life, your life, and every other person's life are the greatest gifts that any of us will ever receive. And even though it often seems like you have to give up, God's going to give you a new day that's going to be yours and yours alone. So hang in there, a new day will dawn.

I AM CROSSING THE NIGHT

Spencer Edmund Foxworth

Evening now, and dark. Outside I can see the sun fading fast behind the blue hills, pulling the last light from the land. A cool wind has come up, and it moans in the hollows of the house. This is a time for turning inside myself.

Things have not been like they used to be. The past year has seen a crashing down of stability and security in every aspect of my life. From morning to night, my life has changed my habits, my outlook, my friends. I know that change is natural, but it is hard, and it hurts.

Is it college? Is it the dissolution of past relationships? Is it the repeated testing and retesting of my values? Is it my over-sensitivity to the problems of our world? On the surface, it is all of these things that affect me. But these are only symptoms of what lies beneath. I sense that the problem runs deeper, like cancer.

I see my reflection in the window and it disgusts me. My face stares back and mirrors my grimace. I am too tired, too exhausted; there are lines appearing in my brow where there should be none. Behind my shadowed eyes lie more darkness and pain. Pain that keeps me up late at nights like these, that sets me against myself.

I see fear. I am afraid of hating myself. I am afraid of being alone. I am afraid people will look at me and laugh. I am afraid of apathy. I am afraid of dying with my life's work yet unfinished. I am so afraid of having dreams and then losing them, never driven, never to know the passion in my hands.

I am afraid . . . it seems to me that I walk a thin line between self-discipline and self-derision. Out of all my fears, this scares me the most. Why is it that I must save me from myself? What is it that divides me?

I look outside. The stars are out, bright beautiful fires dotting the great velvet curtain of the night sky. If I stand up and look past the black shadowy shrubs outside the window, I can see into forever.

These words are difficult to write but they flow faster now. Something heavy is slipping away from me.

Yet I breathe in it, I eat in it, I awaken into it. This world bears down upon me every hour of every day of my life—its concerns, its pressures, its expectations, its ignorance. I am part of it and it shackles me like a slave master.

Pain and lost purpose ride the streets of this world. In TV commercials and parental pressures and friendly advice, the voice of society is ceaselessly chanting to act a certain way, think a certain way, live a certain way. On all fronts of my being I am assaulted.

But I have found it easier. The chanting is still there, as it probably always will be, but its effect on me is subdued. I begin to feel the fear fade away.

Because it really isn't a matter of changing myself. The being that is me is basically unchanged—has been since I was young. My personality is the same as it was when I was four. The division that sets me apart arose when I started to listen to the voices telling me how to live. I was utterly happy until I began to shape myself according to society. That is when unhappiness and disgust were born. I wanted one thing; my world wanted another.

I became too exhausted to go on like that, fighting myself at every turn. I wanted to live again. I try to remember when this realization hit—six months ago? Six hours? It really doesn't matter. What is important is that it happened. I became aware that my fear was a reaction to external influences. In this awareness I discovered what had been lost.

So I fall back. I rise up. I become distant and watch the pressures and expectations of my culture from far off. I ask myself, will it matter in five years? More and more the heavy chains slip away from my ankles.

Get a real job, people say to me. Put down your pen and quit writing your worthless poetry and face reality.

No! I will not stop. I write to live and I will never stop. Life is too majestic and humanity is too tragic and beautiful to stop recording the stories of my people. I will not waste the short time I have here on cheap desperate competitions against one another. I have better things to do with my life.

This is not a denial of society, as some people might say, nor is it an estrangement from it. It is a dance back into life, into the things that really matter: relationships, internal strength, belief in greater powers. It is a letting go of uselessness and a setting of priorities. It is taking what is good from society and leaving the rest. It is me looking at my fears and seeing no basis for them. My dreams, with nothing to block them, become more clear. I am beginning to understand that I can live in this world and set my dreams in it without compromising my beliefs, without being a part of the pain and lost purpose. I can look inside now without so much revulsion toward what is there. Passion for life, laughter at its peaks and valleys, hope in the future is slowly restored.

And I begin to lose a bit of the hurt, day by day.

I want to lead a unique life—I try to, at least. I write poems late at night and early in the morning, walk barefoot through rainstorms, pay attention to lunar phases, stay away from TV, paint watercolors, eat cereal with a fork. It's the small things that help keep me subtly different, objective, at peace. I believe I would go mad if I were to attack the problem all at once—it's just too big. But gradually, step by step, the road is turning, and I am coming around.

And finally, it is morning. Where the sun fell twelve hours before, it is still purple, but in the east the soft spread of dawn glows. I'm tired, but not exhausted; all night I wrote these words, sometimes ploddingly, sometimes with anger. It's okay now. The words are out and I've touched my fear, faced the fountainhead of division. When I see my reflection, it won't be all that bad anymore. I think to myself, it's okay now. I've come home.

OBSTACLES

Maura

There are many obstacles in life we all must overcome. Some are easier to handle than others. Some we struggle through within ourselves; other times we use the strength from others to help us along the way.

My particular obstacle was something only I could overcome. My problem challenged my heart, mind, and soul. It took all I had, and more, to overcome it and continue on to be who I am today. A few years ago, I lost all of my self-esteem. On and off for two years, I struggled through times of loss and desperation. I felt completely alone, not even having myself to help me figure out what was going on.

I'm not exactly sure what sparked these years of pain. There were many things that probably led to it. When I think back and try to remember what happened to me, the most vivid memory is a black cloud of fear. There I was, afraid and alone. I was alone because I shut everyone out. I had no friends. Nothing could get inside of me because I thought everything would hurt me. Everything was painful, including my emotions.

I am sure that as you read this, you are confused. Well, that is what I was. I thought I had no friends, but I had quite a few. I thought I was stupid, but I got straight A's. I thought I was untalented, but I started on a state-tournament basketball team. I thought I was useless when I really was not.

All of these confused emotions made me lose who I was. Adolescence got me by its claws and would not let go. I was trapped with no way out. I can remember just curling up into a ball and crying because that was all I could do for a while. I truly thought of myself as ugly, stupid, and useless. Nothing positive came from my mouth, and I never thought a positive thing about myself.

What can be really damaging about this situation is never coming out of it and being OK with yourself, never realizing your potential as a person. Fortunately, this was not my case. As time went on, I began to accept myself. What really brought me out of this time was the love and support of family, new friends, and teachers. These people helped me to realize my successes. From here, I was able to view myself better. I wasn't afraid or in pain anymore.

This all didn't happen that quickly though. Still today I have to snap myself out of low times and make myself accept who I am. I do this by telling myself all I have accomplished and all the possibilities life has.

I have decided that everything in life has a purpose. I really hated those years of pain, but I'm glad they happened. Now I am a stronger individual. I can be a good friend to others and myself. I now take my weaknesses as a chance to improve and use my strengths to pull me forward. I realize now that having high self-esteem is very important. It is something that can only come from within yourself. You have to want it, you have strive for the rewards it gives you. Whenever I see people with low self-esteem, I want to tell them how much of life they are missing. I really wish I could do those two years over again.

Overall, now I am a very happy person. I smile, something I didn't do for quite a while. I am proud to say that problems don't knock me down any more and they help me move forward. I understand what others may be going through because I've now seen both sides of the bridge, low self-esteem to very high self-esteem.

I thank God every day for giving me a strong enough heart to endure these years of pain. I'm glad that now I can look back on this time as yet another blessing in disguise. I'm grateful that today I am OK with life and all I can accomplish.

Life is a marvelous thing. Enjoy every minute. It sounds corny and unnecessary to say, but it couldn't be closer to the truth, and not all of us understand this.

BLACK DAYS GONE GRAY

Elizabeth Neil

I could overdose on some sort of drugs, or I could run the car with the garage door closed and hopefully die of carbon monoxide poisoning. What about slitting my wrists? No, too messy. I still want my body to look halfway decent when they find me. My mind searched for other ideas when a voice inside my head interrupted my brainstorming, screaming, "Are you crazy? You know you'll never go through with it! You're only sixteen. You have the rest of your life ahead of you." And what a life I had. I practically lived inside my bedroom, with my door always locked, and music as my only companion. I suppose I could be mistaken for a mole, constantly living in the dark. Sure I had friends, but it was never enough. Whenever I was invited out, I usually made up some idiotic excuse, and ended up spending the evening alone in my bedroom. I reached the point where I dreaded Friday and Saturday nights because I would have to think of another excuse for backing out of plans.

No one ever thought anything was wrong with me. How could they? On the outside, I was a normal high school teenager with a decent group of friends, good grades, and involved in school activities. Inside, I was a complete wreck. At night, I would cry myself to sleep, even if I wasn't sad. I just felt better if I cried. During the day, I walked around school with a stupid fake grin plastered on my face. I was like a robot with my friends and family. Every feeling I had was blocked out, and I would automatically react how they expected I would. Fake smiles and enthusiasm started to get easier with more practice.

One day after school, I just lost control. I had so many feelings built up inside of me, I felt like I was going to explode. I paced back and forth across my room, trying to decide what to do. My throat tightened into a hundred knots and my eyes caught sight of a bottle of pills on my desk. I could take them and at least it would take away the pain for awhile. Then I jumped back into reality. I told myself: "I would be fine, just like I always am. My parents think I'm fine. So do my friends. So why don't I feel fine?" I started to become fascinated with death, plotting out more ways to die, intrigued by different people who have committed or attempted to commit suicide.

I dreamed of becoming anorexic. Not because I wanted to lose weight, but because I liked how people looked with toothpick legs and tight skin. This could be another way to slowly destroy myself, hopefully increasing the risk of death. For weeks on and off, I wouldn't eat breakfast or lunch, until it became a habit to skip these meals. It was fun trying to see how long I could go without eating, sort of like a game of "Truth or Dare." This was when I started thinking that this isn't normal. It wasn't normal to wish to become anorexic or to plot out my death, knowing what song I would play when I died. I actually felt scared. I was scared because while I wanted to die, a small part of me hoped I could improve my life.

The days seemed longer after I realized there was obviously something wrong with me. I just couldn't handle anything anymore. I used to be in total control, and now I thought about death to solve my problems. I tried to be rational and look at the good things happening in my life, but it was impossible. I couldn't tell my friends because I didn't want to risk scaring them off or revealing my secrets, but inside, my heart felt like it was breaking.

Emotionally, I wasn't stable. One minute, I would be fine, to a certain extent, the next minute in tears. I worried that if my parents found out, they would put me in some institution with a bunch of crazy people. Wait. Was I one of those crazy people?

It's hard to get up in the morning and try and face the world, but I am trying. It's sort of like alcoholism. Once the alcohol is taken away, what's the use of living life? Without the alcohol there is nothing. For me, trying not to think about ending my life was hard because I didn't know what to do with the time I had. I started realizing that death wasn't the answer to something I couldn't handle, but I didn't know what was.

Every day I am faced with situations I can't control and I have to take life one day at a time, cherishing every moment. I look at people who have cancer, another disease, or an injury. They have no choice about how long they want to live. Life is up to me. This was when my black days started fading to gray. Hopefully, my days will become a white so bright that the rest of the world will know that life is worth living.

TO WHOM IT MAY CONCERN
Matthew David Byrne

For a long time, right before it rained, I would feel lonely. As a false dusk enveloped the world beyond my window, I would sit alone, enveloped in the darkness of my own thoughts. While the clouds wept outside, on the inside I, too, wept. I noticed that tiny rivulets of water ran off of cars and cut across the debris littered streets. I was able to understand a rainy day. Sometimes I felt washed-out, too worn away by my many worries and responsibilities. Before long, my own tears fell like raindrops as I, too, tried to cut through the trash that littered my world. Many times I'd wander in the rain, feeling the cold on my face and hands. I needed that cold and wetness to remind me that I was still alive. While the rain hid everyone in their homes, I was left to wander with my thoughts. And if there were people who braved the rain, I was always saved from the shame of my tears because I knew they would be disguised by the raindrops.

My darkness came in the first few months of my freshman year in high school. I was lost. Lost in the halls, in my classes, at parties, and within myself. One minute I was one person, the next I was another. I began to get paranoid and depressed. Others began to prey on my vulnerability. For a long time I feared trusting anyone, always thinking about how they had or were going to use my trust against me. A few incidents of juvenile teasing caused me to curl up and sit alone in a shadowed corner. Continually I was picked on and ridiculed. I always thought those cutting words were right and that I was a nothing. I was in desperate need of direction and more importantly, happiness.

I was an A student and an average athlete. Socially, though, I was backwards. When it came to females, I was even more backwards. I did not realize that people wouldn't want to be with me if I couldn't even stand to be with myself. The inner turmoil began to show itself on my face and in my actions. Instead of grasping life, I tended to hide myself away at home on the weekends. When Monday rolled around, I pretended my life was full of excitement and that I was a man of action. From the bits of conversation I overheard, I could convince almost anyone that I had gone to "the party" or seen "the game." In reality, I was a boy who was afraid, lonely, and insecure. I had no desire to confront nor overcome the shyness and fear within me. The chasm grew wider for a couple of months. It was not until I stopped and began to think about more than myself that the troubles around me grew grotesquely frightening.

What I saw scared the hell out of me. People I used to consider friends were no longer even recognizable. Alcohol and drugs warped personalities and rearranged priorities. Breaking all the rules and fitting in was all that seemed to matter. No one seemed to care, and many times they literally said so. I could only hang my head. Whether I did so in shame or in fear of contact with others is still unknown to me. Somehow I survived the burst of depression and anxiety that followed. There were days, though, when I couldn't eat, sleep, think, or even talk. In my shoe box full of memories I still have one of the suicide notes I wrote. Life simply had no meaning or purpose and I couldn't take it any longer.

I clearly remember the day I saw the first ray of the light of hope. It was a dreary winter afternoon and I sat alone in the center of my room reading a book about character types and temperaments. My world was spiraling downward into oblivion and I had no way to stop it. I looked, felt, and acted depressed. Suicide took on a look of glorious and ultimate freedom. Every day was struggle to fit in and to find my own identity at the same time.

A light snow had begun to fall and I looked out into the calm curtain of white that was created. It was then that I saw the truth. Just as every snowflake is unique, so too is every person. I realized that at one time or another, we all struggle to be accepted. My problem lay in the fact that I always felt sorry for myself because I was having a hard time at it. I did not think anyone cared or understood. I thought I was a freak, fighting a lost cause, alone.

My friends showed me that for all the differences we possess, there are still a lot of struggles we fight in common. One of them is the battle for identity. I was not alone, yet I was still unique. I had found stable ground and a firm foothold to begin my journey into rebirth. Light poured into my darkness.

To my utter surprise, people gave me a chance. In all my hatred and fear toward the world, I couldn't believe there were still people out there who cared and were willing to look further. Suddenly I had a reason to get out of bed in the mornings. Life finally had a direction—forward.

Slowly but surely I began to find a place and name for myself. I stood up and was counted. I raised my voice and spoke my mind. I became something. For the first time in a long time I had reasons to laugh and real reasons to cry. Instead of fearing what was going on around me, I either tried to change it, or let it go. I was my own person. All this because a small pocket of people saw that I was more than just another name and face. They saw me.

Day by day I spoke and joked with others. I opened my ears and eyes to all the possibilities and probabilities. Activity and thought expelled depression. Poems, music, sports, and even females began to enter my life. With a little pushing and prodding from my friends I began to find happiness again. The darkness was lifted even more.

I realize now that I owe my sanity and my life to my friends. They were either kicking me in the butt or telling me everything was going to work out fine. They showed me self-worth and led me on a path to identity. I do not dare claim that I completely know who I am, but they gave me the opportunity to at least try to find out. In all the darkness that I had created for myself, I had missed the point. Life isn't all about money, cars, parties, or fitting in. Life's about being comfortable, happy, and most of all, loved. They helped show me that.

Thanks Emma, Dennis, James, Amy, Emily, Stephanie, Kelly, and Lisa. You're simply the greatest friends anyone could ever have. I love you all.

PREGNANCY

for the country's

ixed. While there

vices to assit street

en table, her sitting,

ock, the interrogation began

me control over his future

~~tional~~ ~~behavior~~ ~~learned~~ set in a

~~ptured~~

~~their arms~~ I

~~always so much~~ here in

~~themselves~~

when he hit me. I'd

~~and he would~~

lying in the hammock, th

PREGNANCY

Karla Williams ends her essay with these words: "I think having a baby so young doesn't mean you are wrecking your life; it just means that you have to grow up a lot faster." Her story leads up to these words, and we feel in them a kind of wistfulness, a recognition of what she has lost, being a mother so young. Both she and Victoria sum up their situations well, giving us the details of their lives, the problems in their families, and the reactions of their friend.

For Victoria, her pregnancy was part of a larger story of difficulties within her family. She tells us about these problems and what it means to have a child at fourteen. When her dad and her uncle try and make her get an abortion she leaves them forever. Her story is filled with a myriad of problems and with her own courageous struggle to overcome them.

We read so much about teenage pregnancy these days. We hear so many solutions and condemnations, so much blaming and shaming. After reading what Karla and Victoria go through, and how they understand what they have lost, we appreciate the complexity of their situation with more compassion than we had before. Solutions do not seem so simple any more.

FAMILY DIFFICULTIES

Victoria Humphery

My story is about my family and how we have difficulties in our lives concerning us together. I found out I was pregnant in the summer of '92. There were a lot of problems about my pregnancy. On my mom's side of the family, half of the people had happiness and joy in their hearts for me. But the other half was mad and angry. They thought I was too young to have a baby at my age. I was twelve and a half then; I'm fourteen now.

Since everyone in my family knew except my dad, my mom had to look for him. When she found him, she told him I was pregnant. He gave my mom his phone number so I could call him and we could talk. Now I had not seen my Dad since I was three, and he had just decided he could jump back into my life when he found out I was pregnant. I called him and we talked about all kinds of things. We had a lot of things to catch up on. After we talked, he wanted to see me. I went and saw him for the first time in nine years. When he saw me, he couldn't believe how big I was and that I was pregnant. He had all kinds of feelings inside that he wanted to let out. But he didn't. He just let some of them out. He let out the feeling that he was angry, mad, kind of happy, and that he was ashamed that his twelve-year-old was pregnant, because no one in his family had had a baby at such a young age.

So he had had his chance to express his feelings, and it was time for me to express mine. I was hurt, frustrated, sad, and unhappy for the simple fact that he left me and never wrote me a letter, never sent anything on my birthday, and never bothered to call. I was old enough to understand why he had left me so young; it was because he was ashamed of what he had done to my mom and me.

So he thought he wasn't good enough to be my father anymore. But I was still hurt and angry because he still could have wrote or sent me something or anything for my birthday. I forgave him because now he could catch up on what he left behind.

We kept seeing each other and he came over to see how I was, but he still was mad and he tried everything in his power to try to keep me from having my baby. My dad and my uncle even planned to get me an abortion. I was still in my early months so they thought they could do it. I told my dad to stay away from me and so he did.

Soon my uncle and I began to have problems. He was being a pain. A couple of months went by and I was about seven months in my pregnancy. I was asleep in my bed and woke up to the sound of arguing and loud talking. It was my mom and my uncle who were fighting. My uncle had just been ironing when they began to fight. My mom hit my uncle and he threw my mom on the bed and hit her in the face with the iron. The iron was real hot and he put the iron on her body and burned her arm and chest. She was bleeding from her face and her skin was falling off her chest and arm. I called 911 and the ambulance came and took my mom and me to the hospital. They took my uncle to jail and my mom had second-degree burns and they had to give her stitches in the face. They said that she could go home and put cream on her body. She had to exercise her arm and have somebody at home with her to help. Since I was pregnant and couldn't help her, my cousin had to come and stay for awhile.

My mom was still in pain. She would have nightmares about being in bed and the bed was on fire and she couldn't get out. At night when she had the nightmares, she would wake up in a cold sweat and when morning came I would catch her looking at her scars and crying right then and there. I knew that there were a lot of bad feelings that she was having inside, so I would ask her if she wanted to talk about it. She would start to cry when she told me how she felt. She felt angry, hurt, in pain, hate, and she felt like she wanted to kill. But for me not to cry, I told her that it will be alright and that she didn't have to feel like she wanted to kill. Also I said that God had a place for people who did bad things to other people and I said "You can forgive, but never forget."

It was almost time now for me to have my baby. My mom was there but she was still in pain from the burns. Soon I had my baby and he was a seven-pound, fourteen-ounce baby boy. My mom got well and my son is now fifteen months. My dad is still in Minnesota, but I don't know where he is. My uncle is staying with a friend. I am going to school at Juvenile Horizons, and we are all very happy.

TEENAGE PREGNANCY

Karla Williams

Pregnancy can change anyone's life. It changed mine as a teenager. I got pregnant when I was 16 years old. I had been seeing my boyfriend for two and a half years before I got pregnant. When I found out that I was pregnant, I was in total shock. I did not know if I should have an abortion, put it up for adoption, or keep the baby. I didn't think that I could abort the baby or give the baby away because I would never forgive myself. I also was afraid that the father would leave me if I decided to keep the baby.

I thought about it long and hard and decided to keep the baby. I knew that it was going to be hard, but I thought I'd try it anyway for the baby's sake.

I knew that when I walked by people, they would stare. I felt very uncomfortable when I started showing. Some people acted like they had never seen a pregnant teenager before. I felt that my relatives wouldn't like me any more and my friends' parents wouldn't want me to hang around their teen because I was pregnant. Eventually I got used to it and just ignored them.

I thought that my mom was going to kill me when I told her. When I did tell her I think she was more concerned than angry. I think she felt this way because she also got pregnant when she was sixteen years old and she knew how I felt, what I was thinking, and knew what I was experiencing.

If my mom hadn't been there for me I don't know what I would have done. It's like my mom was in my corner cheering me on. I would think to myself my mom made it so can I. My mom didn't make me feel like I did anything wrong, and she didn't point her finger at me. That made me feel a little better about the pregnancy.

Toward the end of the pregnancy, my mom started to get excited. The whole family did. They all had smiles every day asking, "When are you going to have that baby?"

Finally on July 10, 1992, at 12:45 p.m., I had a little boy. My mother couldn't be there because she had to work, but the baby's father was there. He stayed there for the whole delivery. He even cut the umbilical cord. He was excited, and I was in pain, but when I saw that little boy I fell in love and all the pain stopped. My boyfriend and I named him Jeremy. He weighed six pounds, fourteen ounces.

I was nervous and scared after that wondering what was going to happen because I didn't know anything about raising a child. After Jeremy was brought home, my mother helped out a lot. She watched him when I needed a break and helped me with any questions I had.

After getting used to being a mother I noticed that I didn't have as many friends as I did before. It's like they just forgot about me or they just had better things to do. It took some time to accept not going out as much, not having sleep-overs, and not doing the fun things I used to do as a teenager. I had to give up most of my teenage activities. When I realized most of my friends went on with their lives, I decided to settle down and get on with my life such as schooling, getting a good car, and finding a nice home to live in.

Because of my pregnancy and taking care of my son, I am behind in my schooling about two years. Being a teenage mom and trying to go to school is very hard. First I had to find a baby-sitter for Monday through Thursday, and I had to come up with money to pay the baby-sitter—plus do my homework, clean house, cook, and do the laundry. If my son is sick I'm the one who misses school because of it. In addition to my daily school schedule, I am taking two night classes and plan to attend summer school in an effort to catch up. It's not easy, but I've been giving it my best. I now plan to graduate from Willmar Area Learning Center and would like to go to college afterward.

As a single teen mother I think I'm doing okay financially. If I ever needed money, my mother would always help me out and that helped the most.

I think having a baby so young doesn't mean you are wrecking your life, it just means that you have to grow up a lot faster.

IMMIGRANT EXPERIENCES

for the country's
ixed. While there
vices to assit street
n table, her sitting,
ck, the interrogation began
ne control over his future
lying in the hammock, the

IMMIGRANT EXPERIENCE

If we have forgotten, the immigrant experience in this country is still a vital and important part of our culture, strength, and hope. In the seven essays in this section we learn about this experience from the viewpoint of young people who have recently arrived in the United States—from Laos, Russia, Liberia, Chile, and Saudi Arabia. Their stories are filled with the difficulty of transition, the clash of cultures, and the tension with parents who are used to different ways in a different land.

Tong Thao writes about a harrowing canoe ride, opium overdoses to keep babies quiet, and the necessity for silence in order to save his life and the life of his family.

Endu uses the metaphor of coming out of a mother's womb to describe how it felt to move from her own homeland Bahrain, an island southeast of Saudi Arabia, to the United States. She describes how shocked she was by the high school students she encountered and how great the cultural divide seemed to her.

In Liberia, an anonymous young woman had to flee her hometown in the middle of the night. She saw townspeople murdered all around her and escaped by eating edible roots, drinking dirty water, and walking for days to cross the border into the Ivory Coast. Like the others, her story shows the resilience of a young woman and her family and the trauma of starting life over.

In an exceptionally moving essay, Khieo Souvannavong describes the clash between her parent's expectations as Laotian Americans, and her own desires and hopes as a student in an American high school. In one exchange with her mother Khieo says:

"With anger and frustration inside of me I wanted to yell out how I was feeling inside. But that would be disrespectful to her and bring shame for my family . . . ."

She writes that she is living on her own now and the final words of her story break our hearts with their sorrow.

An anonymous young woman of Hmong descent from Laos, describes the situation in her country that led her to come to the United States. In this essay she tells of racism and violence that she encountered in the cities here. She ends her essay with a moving statement of pride in her culture and a resolve to do her best.

Daniel Gittsovich came from Russia when the economy there started to collapse. He centers his essay on what he considers his four major problems: He talked differently, looked different, was the wrong religion, and he was too honest. His is a fascinating explanation of how one young man overcame the challenges of moving to a new country.

Finally, an anonymous author writes about his life in Chile where he was abused and finally sent to a shelter. From this shelter he was adopted by a family in Minnetonka. He writes from the Juvenile Center where he was sent after he shot another young man. I included his story in this section because it started in another country, and the transition to a new culture worsened his situation. His essay could have appeared under the section on abuse or family problems. It is a complicated and difficult one to read.

All these stories are fascinating in the way they show the tenacity of young Americans new to this country. After reading this section, it is clear how varied, rich, and complicated our own country can be, and how important new citizens are to our expanding knowledge of the world.

THE TURNING POINT OF MY LIFE

Tong R. Thao

In the summer of 1984, I escaped with my family from a country filled with oppression and destruction, a country where our lives were constantly in danger, a country where there was no hope and no dreams. I escaped from Lao.

After the fall of the Royal Lao government to the Vietnamese Communists and their allies—the local Pathet Lao, every Hmong man's life was in danger. The reason for this is that the communists were determined to wipe out all Hmong men who had fought against them as soldiers for the U.S. Central Intelligence Agency. Because my father was one of these soldiers, we were constantly fleeing from one village to the next, trying to avoid capture.

Finally, there were no more villages, and no place in Laos left to hide. But there were rumors that some people had tried to escape to Thailand. These rumors said that almost everyone who tried to get there ended up being shot dead or wounded on the banks of the Mekong River—the boundary between Laos and Thailand—and only a handful of families had made it across to the other side, to Thailand and freedom. Although these rumors frightened everyone, even my dad, he was determined to get us out of the country so that we children could be educated and could live a life free from war and communist terror. But really, we didn't have any more choices left. We had to go.

So one dark summer night in June, 1984, I found myself waiting with my family and my uncle's family by the banks of the Mekong River, staring across the distance at Thailand. Everyone was told not to make any noise, because communist soldiers were constantly patrolling the river banks.

In the silence, I couldn't hear anything or feel anything except the beating of my own heart. After a while, though, my baby nephew started coughing. My older brother tried to cover his son's mouth, but the cough kept getting worse. Finally my brother gave him opium to eat, so that he would go to sleep and not make any noise. Usually children who were given opium ended up dead from an overdose, but we were lucky. My little nephew just went to sleep.

The next thing I knew, I found myself crouching inside a small canoe as it drifted slowly to the Thai shore. Fortunately it didn't sink, because it was very small and it had little cracks on the bottom so that water would seep into it. During the whole crossing, my mother constantly dipped the water out, but she dipped very, very, quietly, so that the soldiers guarding the shore wouldn't hear. We made it safely to Thailand. We were free.

That canoe ride on the Mekong River was the turning point of my life. If I hadn't taken it, I might be dead by now, or working for the communists. I'm glad my parents brought me to this country, where I can have hopes and dreams, and not just tears.

COMING TO AMERICA

Endu

When I first decided to come to America, it was in the summer of '90. I had just finished my eighth-grade year in Bahrain, an island southeast of Saudi Arabia. My brother and I flew to the U.S. for a summer vacation. Destination: Minneapolis, Minnesota.

I had a great summer vacation with my family, but when it was time to go back home, I couldn't. The tension between former U.S. president George Bush and Iraqi leader Saddam Hussein had gotten so thick that a day had not gone by without the words "Desert Storm" sliding off people's tongues.

When I realized I couldn't go back home, I had no choice but to find a new life here. I had to make a fresh start, find a new school, new friends, and a new beginning. It was like coming out of a mother's womb, like a baby having to face a different world than the one he or she was used to in her womb.

I enlisted in a high school that my brother Solomon had chosen for me by looking through the phone book. He said it was temporary and was so conveniently located, only five to ten minutes from my house. I was only about a day late for the beginning of the school year from the other kids, but I doubt even if I was there for orientation, it would have made a difference.

It was very hard to adapt to the "American Way of Life" since I had already had to adapt to the British way of life since I was three. I spoke a different English from the people around me, and it seemed more of a correct way to speak. I didn't use any slang words nor did I know any, and I never shortened my words from words like cannot to can't. It was just the way I was, and it was hard for the kids to also get used to me. They often thought I was stuck up, and that was why I spoke with a different accent.

Then during my freshman year I tried out for cheerleading, thinking that I would finally make some friends. But boy was I wrong! I mean don't misunderstand me. I did meet some very nice people, but, on the other hand, I did meet some very unpleasant people. This didn't bother me too much because I knew I still had three more years to make friends.

Then there was the cultural difference. At my old school, it was definitely a no-no to wear make up to school or talk back to your teachers. But here all those things seem acceptable. And then, the biggest shocker for me was when kids sat in class with their feet on their desks. I think that American teachers are more lenient than British teachers, and because of this, students seem to control the running of a class.

Another large obstacle that I had to overcome was having to deal with living without my parents. Because my parents have a life of their own in Bahrain, they couldn't come and live with me, so I lived with my brothers and sisters. I do see my parents at summer vacations or Christmas time, and I talk to them whenever they call to say "Hi."

I had to learn to grow up faster than I was scheduled to because I didn't have my mum there doing my laundry, cooking my meals, and rolling my socks into neat little balls. I started to think for myself and just plainly hit responsibility head on.

Now that I'm 17, it has gotten a little easier to fit in because I've been so exposed to the American culture. Sometimes it's hard to go to school with Americans and come home to an Ethiopian family. Now, all I have to do is to try to adjust to the American life in the real world after high school and on to college.

I'll be graduating from high school in a few months and as soon as I'm done with that, I plan on going to college pursuing a career in law. I think now that I'm getting older, my family (especially my parents) will expect me to grow into the Ethiopian culture.

My parents come to visit every so often and when they do, they always brag about how proud they are that I'm their "American child." Since I've put all my energy to fit in with other American kids, I'm starting to lose my Ethiopian roots. I guess now that I've learned to fit in a culture, I'm going to have to go through the whole thing all over again to fit in with my family.

It's really difficult and confusing to go from a British culture to an American culture and now to an Ethiopian culture. Now I'm back on the roller coaster. HERE WE GO AGAIN!!!

MY EXPERIENCE DURING THE LIBERIAN CRISIS

Anonymous

INTRODUCTION

This paper is all about my experiences that I went through during the crisis in Liberia. Liberia is located on the west coast of Africa. She got her independence on July 26, 1847.

I want to share with my friends all the ordeals that I went through. No matter how important you are, when it comes to war, you are treated as the lowest person. Also, you will get to know what it's like leaving your home, and then to later find out that you will never return home.

But despite all these difficulties, be proud of your country, and help to rebuild it one day.

MY STORY

I still remember that Tuesday night of November 1990, when my sisters and I were preparing for school on Wednesday. We were so excited about returning to school after our Thanksgiving Day's break. We could not wait to see our friends. We went through our devotion as usual, and everyone went to bed.

About two o'clock that Wednesday morning, I woke up to use the restroom. I heard a lot of cars going up and down the street. When I went back in my room, I woke my sisters up, and told them the news about the cars. But no one believed me. We all went back to sleep. All of a sudden, our father rushed into our room to tell us that the soldiers had taken over Bong Mines (where we lived) and that we had to leave as quickly as possible. Everyone got so nervous, we did not know what to do. We packed few jeans in our back packs, and rushed out of the house, thinking that we would return as soon as possible. When we got on the road, I was very amazed about thousands of civilians were on the road, everyone running for their lives. Babies, women, men—even the pets were running for their lives. Some people were fainting, some got hurt. Some kids lost their parents in the crowd. By now, the shooting got worse. The enemies were getting closer every minute. We were just going, not knowing where. We walked through the bushes for what seemed like hours, without food. We ate on any root that was edible, drank from any creek that we came across.

We had to stop at checkpoints where we were checked by both male and female solders. If they were satisfied with you, they allowed you to go. If not, they detained you, and later killed you. People were being killed because they were not of certain ethnic group or because they spoke a different dialect other than what they wanted you to speak. We had to empty our suitcases on the ground for inspection. And these soldiers would deliberately take your things from you without even asking you for it. There was nothing that you could do. They were in power. Your relatives were killed right before you, but what would you do? If you tried to help they would tell you that since you wanted to be nice, your life will be taken away next.

I got so sick on the highway, from drinking all the dirty water and eating all the roots. When we finally got to the border between Liberia and the Ivory Coast, the airplane started dropping bombs and a lot of people got wounded. My cousin's face got wounded from the bombs. There were certain chemicals in it that were leaving marks on people.

We managed to cross the border and got to the Ivory Coast, where we started life all over from scratch. With the help of our relatives from the United States, we were able to survive the struggle. We were able to attend school, to forget about all that we passed through.

I should have been out of high school by now, but because of the war, I am still in high school. But thank God that I am still in school. Most of my friends who would have been out of high school got killed. I hope to complete my studies and go back home one day to help rebuild my country. There's nowhere like home.

In my conclusion, I will like say that despite the crisis, I am still proud to be a Liberian.

RUN AWAY

Khieo Souvannavong

Back in Laos, families are different from families in America. Laotian families have so many rules and expectations. In school you have to follow directions or else it's the spanking on the butt. If not that, it would be some other horrible punishment. In families, daughters have very little freedom. The women have to cook, clean, help their mother, and they always have to follow the mothers everywhere they go, even to their friends' parties. If your parents decided that you should get married, there would be a man that your parents would pick for you, and then from there you have to listen to your husband. All of this sounds terrible, but in Laos it doesn't mean anything because every woman has to face this through her life. These rules and expectations are to be followed. If they are not followed, people in the town will not respect you. They might even call you a whore, and then parents and families would feel hopeless and ashamed.

I respect my culture, but there's things that I don't agree with. I have had so many problems since I moved to America.

My first and my last problem began when I was coming back from school. There stood my mom in front of the kitchen sink. "Honey, please don't go out a lot. You know I'm worried about you when you're out," my mom says.

"Okay," I said.

"What's up with this soccer stuff? Do you go everyday to practice and play? Soccer?"

"Yes, Mom!"

With anger and frustration inside of me I wanted to yell out how I was feeling inside. But that would be disrespectful to her, and bring shame for my family that mommy's little girl would do that. So I just decided to go upstairs to my quiet, lonely room. I had been thinking, why is it that my family is so strict? They don't really understand how I want my life to be. Even when I am a little girl growing up in America, things don't get any better in the family.

My oldest brother is the type of guy who doesn't like our family to be put down by any of our relatives. He thinks they all do that, just because they've got a few more things than we do. So he is always telling me, "Get a ride to success and power, you gotta get some education, so people can't stomp on our heads."

I was always afraid of him, because of his strong, threatening words to beat me up if I ever went out with my friends. He thinks they're all bad. I know he would never beat me up. He just threatens me to stay home and out of trouble from the outside world. He wants me to study hard, go to college, stay home, and have no boyfriends. NO LIFE is what I think. I ask myself, "How am I ever going to get through this miserable life?" I pray someday that I'd be born again to some other family where I could have some freedom.

During school, looking at a blank blackboard, I am trying to decide what would happen this time if I lied to my brother, who's always there at my house every time he gets out of work at 4:00 p.m. just to check on me.

"Hey girl, let's go to the Mall today. We'll pick you up at 2:30 p.m. Get ready okay?" Candi says.

"I don't think I can, Candi, maybe next week. I was gone yesterday and I got in trouble from my brother," I said.

"Ooh, I bet that was really bad, I know how that could be. It's been a long time since we have been hanging out last summer. So now everybody wants you to come and hang-out or else they'll be mad at you, and so would I."

"Okay, but only today. It's the last time . . . I think."

After the mall I had a ride home with some friend of mine.

"Okay guys, I'll see ya in school tomorrow."

"Hey, we'll wait for you here for five minutes, in case something happens. Good luck," says Sam.

I walk along the sidewalk to my house thinking hard about what I will say to my brother and my Mom, again.

"Young lady where have you been? We waited here for five hours and you weren't here. Is that what you call soccer practice after school, or are you just giving me another lie!!" my brother yells.

"Look you've been so hard on me for a long time, and you know what? I can't take it no more. I got friends out there waiting for me just to make sure I'll be safe if I come in the house. I can't believe this even is my own home. I'm afraid to come in. I'm eighteen years old! I don't have to take this. I'm leaving. Good-bye mom. I'll always love you, but for you brother, you can get your trashy words and stay out of my life."

From the words I said it made me nervous and choked. From the tears I cried, words couldn't come out right. I felt so empty, and hurt that I had to do this. Then, I felt shame. It wasn't the shame I felt for myself but the shame for my family that they made me do this. I ran out the house and got in the car and left without a trace.

I am now living on my own. I do regret what I've done. But for my own rights, I don't think I have done something wrong. Since then, I've never communicated with any of my family because I don't think it is right for me to talk with them again, I know they're still living in the culture of Laos. I know for me, it's time for me to move on.

STRUGGLE TO FREEDOM

Anonymous

When my family still lived in Laos, I was about one year old. I was young and didn't know what was going on. But my parents told me that at that time there was a war going on. The Vietnamese were taking over Laos. At that time all of the men had to go to the war, including all of the boys age twelve and up. When they went to war they never came home. They had to stay in the jungle. The women provided them with their needs, like food and water. To be able to do this, the women had to get up really early in the morning, like around two or three. They got up, they prepared the foods. After they had finished preparing, they brought the foods to their husband in the jungle.

But the Vietnamese were too strong. The Hmong couldn't fight back because they didn't have enough weapons like the Vietnamese. So the Hmong decided to escape. Escaping was tough for the parents because the husband had to guard the family. Also he had to carry a baby on his back too. Same goes for the mother. She had to carry baby and clothes, foods, etc. If a baby was crying, the parents must give drugs to the baby, to make the baby fall asleep. Some parents gave too much drugs to the baby so the baby died. Some parents got killed during the war so their children became orphans. The Hmong had to hide in the mountains without a lot of food to eat. Some died because of starvation. Even though they were starved and weak, they had to keep on going even during a raining night. If they didn't keep on going the Vietnamese would capture them and enslave them. So some people decided to surrender to the Vietnamese. But some refused to.

Finally, some Hmong people reached Thailand, including us. In Thailand, life was a little bit easier. At that time I was around seven years old. In Thailand, they provided you with some food, but not enough to support the whole family. So my parents had to work too. Life in Thailand is a very scary life too. If the Thai found out that you're not a citizen they'll arrest you and put you in jail. We lived in Thailand for about one or two years, then we came to the United States.

When we got here, in Minnesota, life was not as easy as I thought it would be. There was a lot of stuff the Hmong people had to face, like, racism, prejudice, gangs, drugs, religions, laws, etc. Around that time I was about eight or nine years old. We lived with our cousin for about nine to ten months. Then our cousin took me and my brothers to school. They put me in second grade, my oldest brother in ninth grade, the other brother in sixth grade. At that time neither me or my brothers could speak any English. I don't know about my brothers, but they had a person translate what the teacher said to me. Learning English is not that easy. As you can see, right now my English isn't that good either. You can tell by the way I wrote this letter.

Anyway, let's get back to the story. After a couple of months, we learned how to write our names and some easy stuff, like chair, pencil, paper. Then we moved to live by our own.

When I was in sixth grade, I experienced something that I could never forget. It was Tuesday afternoon, my mom had an appointment to the doctor. So my mom and I took the city bus to the hospital. When we stepped inside the bus, there weren't a lot of people on the bus except a couple of old ladies and two black kids and a white boy. My mom and I sat in an empty seat in the middle. When we got seated the bus started to move. The three kids looked straight at us and laughed. They come and sit behind us and started to make fun of us. They called us "chinks," and one of them said, "Go back to where you came from. You don't belong in here!" I couldn't believe it but I think they were right. Maybe we don't belong here. Even today I still have to face the same situation. So do all of the Hmong people.

But I don't care what people say or think of my culture. I'm proud of my culture. Proud of who I am. I'll prove to them by going to school and do my very best. I'll try my best to learn and work as hard as I can. And I hope that all of the Hmong will do the same as me.

A WHOLE NEW WORLD

Daniel Gittsovich

It all started when one day when the Russian economy started collapsing. The prices began climbing up as the value of the ruble started to fall. I was only ten years old at the time, so I didn't realize what was happening until I noticed that ice cream cost one ruble more than it used to. Later I found out that this was happening because more and more people were moving away to live in countries like the United States and Israel, because they were afraid a civil war would commence.

I was going to a normal Russian public school where no signs of change took place, except for maybe the fact that teachers started talking more about the economy and the future of the country. I didn't really care about money back then. I mean, we didn't have any financial problems, and I got my share of spending money, so actually there was nothing to worry about for me. But my parents were much smarter than I was. They predicted the economy would crash within a year or so, so they decided to move away to America.

I liked the idea even though that meant that I would have to leave all my friends back in Russia. I thought we would all write to each other, so I wouldn't miss them at all. And maybe one day when I had saved up enough money, I would go back to Russia and visit them. And maybe, too, some of my friends could come and visit me some day. So as you can see, all I had were happy thoughts of a wonderful new life in a different country. I was not prepared for the problems that I would have to face in America.

ONE YEAR LATER

As our plane descended from the sky, I was stunned to see a bunch of lit-tle houses and a couple of apartment buildings instead of huge skyscrap-ers. You see I always imagined America as the "Country of Skyscrapers," and I thought every American city had to have one. Our friends met us at the airport. They drove us to the apartment they rented for us, and a half hour later they drove off. I fell asleep immediately after they left. I didn't care what tomorrow would bring. I just wanted to sleep. You prob-ably can't imagine what I felt like, because you have probably never been on a twenty-four-hour plane ride. If you ever were on such a ride, then I feel very sorry for you.

About two weeks later I started going to my new school, and that's when all my troubles began. As soon as I got there I realized that I did not fit in with the rest of the crowd. For example, everyone wore their shirts hang-ing down, but not me. I wore mine tucked into my pants very tightly. I did not know what cool meant. In fact I didn't even know the word exist-ed. You see, in Russia I had to wear my clothes the proper way. In other words, I had to wear my clothes the way my parents told me to.

Another problem was that I spoke with an huge accent, and I spoke a lot, so no one could understand me. Everyone used to tease me about that, and since I didn't know what they were saying, I just smiled back at them like an idiot. That only made them get angry at me, because they thought that I was laughing at them, while I was just extremely confused.

Another problem was that I was Jewish, and whenever someone asked me what religion I was, I told them the truth. The thought of not telling did not even come to my mind. I didn't even think that maybe it would be wise to just tell people what they really needed to know, and no personal stuff.

Lots of people in my school took advantage of my honesty and asked questions that you wouldn't even believe. It took them a while to explain to me what the questions meant, but when they finally did, I answered every question they asked. So as you can see, I had four major problems: I talked differently, looked differently, I was the "wrong religion," and I was too honest.

Of course, I soon realized that no one liked me because of my problems. But since I didn't know how to solve any of my problems, I just kept doing what I was doing before, which was talking and not understanding anything. As time went on, I started losing my accent. I also started understanding what was said to me. I then realized that I had improved my language skills greatly. So now I got rid of one of my problems—language.

As I worked on my language problem I also started working on my wardrobe problem. I asked my parents for some new clothes; they bought me a couple of shirts. They also bought me a pair of shoes to go with my new clothes. This time when my parents said that I had to wear my shirt tucked into my pants, I explained to them the reason why I wanted to wear my clothes hanging out. They agreed that what was the best for me was to wear my clothes the way everyone else did, to fit in with the rest of the kids.

As for the problem with my religion, I decided to ignore the people who teased me about it. To some people I even tried to explain that my religion meant a lot to me and that I was in no way ashamed of it, and if they couldn't accept me the way I was, they would have to just pretend I did not exist. They could ignore me

I never did solve the problem with me talking too much. I am in the principal's office very often, because some teacher sent me out of class for talking.

So as you can see, I solved most of my problems and made some new friends in the process. I also learned to get along with people, even the people who don't like me.

MY JOURNEY FROM SANTIAGO, CHILE, TO MINNEAPOLIS

Anonymous

"Stop, stop. I didn't mean to." (I said this in Spanish, of course, because I was born in Chile.)

My dad hit me across my face. My dad hit me across the face with a stick that he could barely hold in his hand! He made me unconscious for a few minutes. When I woke up and saw my mother she asked what happened to me. I told her, but when she found out, she said, "I don't know what I should do with you." She accused me of causing it, and said that I deserved it. She thought that I did something to cause all this.

A few days passed, something big happened to me. I never thought that it would happen to me. They kicked me out of the house at the age of six and a half. When all this happened, at first I was really scared. I slept in the street about three or four blocks away from my house. I really didn't know what to do. I started stealing to survive. I really wasn't good at it. I got caught a couple of times, but I finally got good at it. I got too good at it. Sometimes I took things without even thinking about it.

A few months passed. I was walking down the street and this guy came up to me and asked me what was wrong. I didn't even know him, but I told him and after we were done talking he took me home. When we got there my mom and my dad were there. The man told me to get out of the house for a minute while he talked to my mom and dad. When he called me back, he told me something about my mom and dad trying to find me. They were trying to find me because they were going to talk to me about me getting adopted. I didn't know what adopted meant at that time.

After a few days passed my mom took me to a bus station. I didn't know what was going on at the time. A man met us there. I didn't know him, but he took me to a shelter, and there is where I met my all so-called adoptive parents. I didn't really like it, but they said that I had to go with them. But at that time my sister was with us. Before I didn't know that my sister was coming with me. I just thought that she was coming to keep me company.

My sister and I stayed at the shelter for a few days, but we still didn't know what was going on. I found out later that adoption meant that we had to have new parents. My sister and I went to the airport, and my sister did not really like it so she was yelling and screaming with anger. They had to force her to the airport. I talked to my sister on the airplane and I told her what I knew about adoption. I didn't know much, but I told her everything that I knew. My sister and I were crying and fell asleep.

We flew to the St. Paul airport. We were wearing shorts and it was during the winter. A couple of people who said they were cousins of the adopting parents came and picked us up. They took us to the house in Minnetonka.

A few days passed. They wouldn't let us go outside because they were afraid we would get lost. During all this time we had a tutor who translated Spanish to English. My new mom took my sister and me shopping and we went to the Minnetonka Mall. We had heard the U.S. was a "free country" so we took things without paying because we thought it was all right. My adopting parents explained that we were Spanish and didn't know anything about the United States.

We went over to the YMCA and when we got there she bought us shorts and a swimming suit. I thought that I knew how to swim and wanted to show off for my sister so I jumped into the deep water and almost drowned myself. We were there for a couple of hours. My adopting dad came and picked us up while my mom went to work. He took me to his factory where he worked. I cut myself with knives there when I tried to juggle them.

I stayed there a year. Everything was going right and all of a sudden it went wrong. It started when we went to their cabin. My sister and I got into a fight and they were hollering at me more than my sister. So I just ran away. It was in Wisconsin. I ran to a city about twenty-five miles away. I was about nine then and I don't think I had ever been to school yet. I ran to the police station. I told them what happened. They laughed at me because they thought it was stupid so they said they would take me back to the cabin. It was about 9:30 and it was dark. We had a shortened vacation I guess, so they took me back to the house in the city. They hit me there.

That was when I ran away down to a park and I slept there for a couple of hours. Then I went back to the house. My parents told me if I hadn't come back they would have called the cops.

I started going to school in Minnetonka. I started fighting everybody. I even started fighting the counselor. I wasn't good in classes and that was very frustrating.

After a while I just started running away from home and coming to south Minneapolis. I met this kid and he was in a gang called Gangsta' Disciples. He showed me how to get respect and be in a gang and show courage and violence. I got caught once doing a break-in. They put me in Juvenile Center and then they said I wasn't well enough to be in the community. They put me in this place called Northwoods. I wasn't doing everything the court wanted me to do. I started to be violent to kids and staff.

They put me in a foster home near Duluth, and while I was in that foster home, I wasn't really doing good there either, so I started robbing places and breaking and entering and also sold drugs. Everybody liked me there, but there was one kid who starting picking on me. I got sick of him "punking" (pushing) everyone, and he started "punking" my girlfriend so I decided to take care of the trouble that I had with him. Somebody sold me a .32 and when he came to a football game, he started pushing me around and hitting me. I brought out the gun. I shot at him once and he started to run away. I shot towards him but I kept missing.

I went home and I didn't really know what to do because I was so nervous about what would happen to me. I came back to school the next week and people cheered me because he had been pushing people around.

It was starting to snow. The snow was mushy—snow and water together. That day I got kicked out of school for mouthing off to a teacher and hitting a student. I was out of school for three days for that incident. Toward the last day, before I was supposed to come back to school, the police came to my house and said I was wanted for shooting and burglarizing. They brought me down to Juvenile Center in Duluth. I went to court the next day. I went and said, "Not Guilty." So they said that I had to come down to Minneapolis Juvenile Center and have a trial. When I got down to Minneapolis I saw a lot of my friends, so I told them what happened. They couldn't find any evidence that I did anything to him because people were on my side because he had mistreated people so much.

I've been in Juvenile Center seven months, and now they're thinking of putting me in a place in Colorado for three years for second-degree assault. Now that I'm thinking what all has happened to me in my life, I have started looking back, and think I should start changing my life because I'm getting older and it could get even harder. I need to get out of gangs. I would like to finish school and go to the University of Minnesota at Duluth. Hopefully, I can have a job where I can help kids not to do the same things that I did. Otherwise I would like to be a radio DJ and tell people things I've learned and that life doesn't have to be so negative. If I can do this, anybody can.

Now I'm looking forward to changing my life and looking forward to a goal that I'm planning for myself.

RACISM AND HOMOPHOBIA

t for the country's
ixed. While there
ervices to assit street
en table, her sitting,
ock, the interrogation began
me control over his future
tical behaviour set in
ptured
their arms I
ways so much late in
when he hit me. I'd
stair and he would hit
lying in the hammock, th

RACISM AND HOMOPHOBIA

These four stories are about the will to keep going. They are about one of the darkest parts of this country: our heritage of racism and its effect on the young people who live here. Dawn, in "The Missing Piece of My Heart," chronicles her life in the United States from kindergarten through high school by means of a series of letters to her biological mother in Korea. In the middle of her story she says:

"I'm starting to forget that I look different from the rest. I think that will be the only way I can get over my being adopted from a different race. "

She struggles with this the rest of the essay, and we struggle with her. By the end, in her last letter to her mother from Korea, we sense a kind of reconciliation for Dawn.

The next story by an anonymous young woman describes her struggle to maintain pride in her culture in the face of racism. Her parents tell her to "look at myself. I have black hair and brown eyes, I am Asian, I'll never be as good as the whites." By the end of the essay we realize that she will not give in but will maintain her racial pride at great expense.

"Not Just Half and Half" is a fascinating description of what it is like to have a Mexican father and a European mother. As this young man says in his opening paragraph:

"It has been a challenge throughout my life to determine what I want to consider myself, instead of others dictating it to me, and facing both the racism that Mexicans and whites encounter."

He takes us on his journey of self discovery and we admire his conclusion that "an even bigger challenge for me is to decide what I am for myself."

Finally a young woman writes openly and honestly about realizing that she is attracted to other women as well as men, about being bisexual, and about accepting this part of herself. She is unflinching in her inspection of her own homophobia and strong in her resolve to continue in being open to all people, including herself.

We know that it is difficult for adults to deal with racism and homophobia, both in themselves and others. We realize after reading this section, then, how tough it is for young adults who are struggling with the normal confusion of growing up, to also fight the constant battle of prejudice in this country.

THE MISSING PIECE OF MY HEART

Dawn

To my real Mommy,
Today was the first day of kindergarten. I hated it, 'cause all the kids made fun of me. I look different then the rest of them. I didn't even know that. All the kids on the way home sang, "Chinese, Japanese, dirty knees look at these!" I started to cry and just kept walking home. I couldn't let my new mommy see me cry, cause she might be mad that I look different too. Do you think she knows I look different from her?
Love, Dawn

Dear Real Mommy,
I'm in second grade now, and I think of you a lot. Did you even love me, or was I really that bad you had to let me get adopted way over here. I don't understand. All the kids think I'm really weird when they find out I have two mommies. My mommy here is really nice and I'm not saying I don't love her, but it just kind of makes me feel bad she couldn't have more real children like my little brother. Some kids still make fun of me, but I try to ignore it. I have some friends that like me even though I'm different.
Love, Dawn

Dear Mom,
I'm in fourth grade now and I like school really well and I have a lot of friends and a nice teacher. No one makes fun of me anymore 'cause they know who I am and what I'm like. And if anyone does make fun of me my friends stick up for me. I still wish I knew about you. Sometimes all my friends and even teachers ask me if I ever want to go back to Korea and find you. I say I don't know. I'm not really sure if you would want to find me 'cause you gave me up and didn't want me. I don't know what to think of you anymore.
Love, Dawn

Dear Real Mommy

I'm in sixth grade now and I'm going into junior high next year. I'm scared, now that I have all my friends here who know me and like me even though I'm Korean. I'm going to have to go through being made fun of all over again. Most of my friends are going to the other junior high. I know this is kind of mean 'cause I don't even know you, but sometimes I get so mad at you. I get mad at you for leaving me these looks, making me look different then the rest. Do you even care that you gave me up to some strangers you didn't even know? I'm not saying they aren't nice. I mean my parents now are really nice to me. I guess I'll never know why you didn't love me enough to keep me.

Dawn

Dear Mom,

I'm in seventh grade and just starting it. It's not so bad. There are kids of different races. I'm starting to forget that I look different then the rest. I think that will be the only way I can get over my being adopted from a different race. I like it 'cause I'm not the only one that looks different. I know this sounds dumb, but I miss you and I almost feel like all of my heart isn't here because I don't have you. I really wonder what you look like? Maybe you were a prostitute and got pregnant, maybe you were too young, maybe you're dead, or maybe you just didn't love me. I do want to meet you someday, but you are to far away.

Love, Dawn

Hi Mom,

Me again, I'm so ugly and just sick of being me. I moved junior highs 'cause a new one was built and was closer to my house. I can't get a boyfriend, 'cause my eyes are so small and no one wants to go out with a chink. I hate being the minority in the mart. I want nothing to do with the Asian race. I want an eyelift, but that costs to much money now. My best friend is beautiful. She's white, has blond hair, and great big green eyes. I'm jealous that she got such big eyes and she's so normal. I try so hard, but I still feel so weird and I just hate looking so different from the rest. It's easy to forget when you don't have to look in the mirror, but when you do it just reminds me of how ugly it is to be different. I think I fit in fine in this school, but I wouldn't blame the people for being racist to me if they were 'cause I do look different than the rest. Maybe that scares them.

I know I'll never be able to meet you. My mom told me that it was pretty much impossible to find you. I still think of you as my secret diary and friend. If someone found out, they'd probably think I'm weirder than I already am. I wish I had you now, 'cause everything now is starting to go wrong at my home. My mom and dad are always fighting with me. Sometimes it is so hard to see them as my mom and dad when I am not even a blood child. My grandmother won't accept me because I'm not a real child. I can't get along with my sister and brother. She is so smart and I can't handle competing with her all the time. I know my parents love her more 'cause she's smart. I've just come to the conclusion that I'm dumb and quit trying to be smart because I'll fail even worse than I thought.

Mom,
I'm so sick of school and everything is going wrong in my life. No one loves me—not even you. I've been joking myself. My whole life is just a joke. I can't go on. It's ninth grade now and I still have never had a boyfriend, I'm only making the "B" honor roll, not the "A" like my sister. Things are worse than they ever were with my father. I just feel so bad that no one loves me. The only friend I have is my very best friend and she's my life. People started spreading mean rumors we were lesbians, but we aren't at all. She likes boys just as much as I do. We can't help it if they don't like us. It makes me so mad that you sent me over here to make your life better and make my life miserable.

It's so hard right now 'cause all I do is cry. My parents think I have some kind of depression and want to send me to a shrink. I can never stop being sad. I have the worst self-esteem. The way I see it is that if you didn't love me enough to keep your very own daughter of your flesh and blood, how can I expect anyone to love me now? You didn't even want me as a baby. I'm just ready to die; that's all I want, to get hit by a car and die. This is your fault 'cause it would have never been this way if you hadn't had given me up. Well, too late now.
Dawn

Mom,
It's me. Sorry I haven't written in awhile. I was so mad at you for the worst reason of all. It's tenth grade now, and we are in first trimester. I just got

back from a place I never want to go again. I was in the hospital. I tried to kill myself and end my life. I was so sad and I couldn't take it anymore. I couldn't take it that you didn't want me, and because of that base feeling I had it all branched off from there and made everything else worse. I was going through a depression and I let it get the best of me. I'm doing better now and I need to get my life back on track because I don't want to do this again and put everyone through this again. That was the most selfish thing I could've done and I feel so bad. I know that you must have loved me enough to let me come to America and have a better life, and put me with some people that really care and love me. I'm truly sorry for living my life blaming it all on you.

I still want to meet you and see what you look like and give you all the time in the world to explain to me why? I really love you.
Love, Dawn

Dear Mom,
Today right now I'm a junior in high school and my life is back together. I have a great future ahead of me. I've learned a lot from all my problems and realized life is too short to blame things on others and live your life filled with regret. I used to regret you giving me up. I now really do realize it was for the best. I never thought my adoption could affect my life so much and hurt me in so many ways. I think as I grow older, the whole issue should get easier, at least I hope so. I know I would like to meet you someday or at least come to where I was born. I'm just starting to accept what I look like now that I have a wonderful boyfriend who thinks I'm beautiful. I really have no idea why, but it helps. Maybe one day we'll meet, but maybe not and if we don't I hope you have a good life, 'cause mine is going much better!
Love always,
Your daughter Dawn

I AM WHO I AM

Anonymous

My life was basically normal when I was younger. My family moved to America when I was one and a half years old. It was a big change for us and we decided to settle in Amarillo, Texas. I lived there for ten years of my life. During that time I became aware that there were many things out in the world for me. I had many strong beliefs. I was an independent and determined child.

When I reached the age of ten, I had many dreams in my head. Whatever they were, my parents still wanted me to be a doctor or a lawyer. If I did not want the same, then they wouldn't support me in anything else. I could never be a doctor. The sight of blood makes my stomach queasy. And being a lawyer would be too much pressure since it's in a courtroom. I wanted to be able to act and play sports and get a scholarship. My parents wanted an academic scholarship for me. They told me to stop day-dreaming and jump back into reality. They told me to "look at myself. I have black hair and brown eyes. I am Asian. I'll never be as good as the whites."

I was angry—angry that out of all people my parents were the ones being racist to me. People have told them so many times that white people were superior to everybody, that they began to believe it, and they tried to get me to believe it too. Well, I wasn't about to be ashamed of who I was. I am proud of my appearance. But Mommy and Daddy just didn't understand that. They told me my goals were too high and I was stupid to ever think I could reach them. So I gave up wanting to act, wanting to play tennis, wanting to be me, so I could please my parents.

To my family I was always the dreamer. I hated what my mother said was women's work—cleaning the house. I loved cooking but that was as far as it goes. My old school was crazy. People always fighting and arguing. There was a group of kids I used to hang out with. One girl was popular and had cool clothes. Most of the girls wanted to be like her. I didn't. Soon they all turned against me. So I made new friends, with people who really cared about me. But still, what I wished for, was to have the future I wanted.

Now we moved from Amarillo to Minneapolis. I couldn't believe all the racism here. Wherever I went, the word "chink" was always around me as if it were printed on my back. They would call me different names like "ricecake" or "riceback." What was wrong with the food we ate? Why do they put it against us? You don't see me calling other people "wetback."

I have overcome the feeling of being discouraged and being lost. I learned that you may not always get what you want. That's why we must compromise. I overcame the silent anger inside of me. I should not let things bother me so much. Keeping too many things hidden isn't very healthy. I have also overcame the impression that I must please others. I learned how to please myself.

NOT JUST HALF AND HALF

Anonymous

My name is Martin Sanchez. By looking at my name, immediately you would guess that I am Hispanic. By looking at me, you would probably guess that I am white. My father is Mexican and my mother is European-American, which logically would make me exactly half Hispanic and half white. But in reality, others consider me whichever ethnic race is more convenient for the given situation. It has been a challenge throughout my life to determine what I want to consider myself, instead of others dictating it to me, and facing both the racism that Mexicans and whites encounter.

As a young child, I experienced many cultural activities and did not even realize it. I had pinatas at all of my birthday parties, sometimes listened to Mexican music, and even spoke Spanish at home. I did not even know what a minority was, much less consider myself one, because I did not think anything of my ethnic household.

By the time I entered junior high, I was finally introduced to the concept of being a minority. It began when counselors urged me to join the Minority Encouragement Program at school. I did, but in my mind I was only "playing along" with the whole ordeal because there would most likely be scholarship money involved. However, I was embarrassed to attend these meetings. I remember trying to avoid telling my teacher where I was going, and even more so I avoided telling the other students in the class. I had no reason to feel that way at the time, but my logic was that it did not really matter what race I was, so the meetings were rather pointless.

The summer between seventh and eighth grade, I was encouraged to join the University of Minnesota Health Sciences Minority Program. For the first time ever, I realized that racism was not just an awful thing of the past, but instead it was alive and well in the present and affecting me daily. The racism that I had never felt up until that point definitely existed; I was just too naive to notice that it was there. Finally I was aware of the racism around me, but as I began high school I wished that I never would have discovered it because it would never go away.

A few months into my freshman year of high school, I was nominated to be part of the royalty at the Homecoming Coronation. I had never before in my life felt race to be such an issue as it was at that time. Voting occurred several times, and with each round I heard new stories about what people had said about me as they cast their ballots. One group of people did not know any of the candidates, and they wanted to make sure that they voted for a minority. They chose to vote for me because they could tell by my name I was what they were looking for. I appreciated the votes, but I wanted them to vote for me because of who I was, not what race I belonged to.

When the day finally came, I entered the gymnasium in my new formal dress to find some people booing because they thought I was white. It did not ruin the moment for me, but I was definitely saddened that such a thing would ever occur. Soon after, I became angry with myself for letting a few ignorant people dampen my spirits. But to this day, all of the coronations I have attended at my school have included some people booing against a person because they are white.

It seems that no matter what race I am considered, racism exists. As a white person I have been pushed in the hallway at school and listened to comments directed at me because I am a "white girl." As a white female, I have been among groups that have received derogatory remarks from strangers about our clothing because it was considered to be appropriate for only black people to wear.

As a Hispanic, I feel left out of society. I am constantly working as hard as I possibly can because I want to have as good a life as a nonminority would have. I also want to excel to disprove the many negative stereotypes about my race.

Society considers me Hispanic, but I cannot say that I truly am. When I speak with my few Hispanic relatives in Spanish, I am afraid because my Spanish is not absolutely fluent. I do not have any Hispanic friends to grow up with and share different cultural experiences. In Spanish class, when the Hispanic culture, traditions, or attitudes are explained, I know more than the average student, but I do not truly know what if feels like to be Hispanic.

It is the Hispanic tradition to throw an elaborate celebration, called a quinceanera, on a girl's fifteenth birthday. I did not have one, but I attended one and enjoyed it a great deal. However, I felt as if I were on the outside looking in, because I did not fully understand the meaning of all of the unique rituals involved.

As I fill out questionnaires, or recently have been filling college information request forms, I am sometimes asked to identify my race. On several forms there has been a "Hispanic" category and "white" (non-Hispanic) category. I cannot honestly check either category because neither of them fully apply to my situation. I do not like being labeled either one, but when faced with a choice, I have to make it. In this situation, I will choose the Hispanic category because that is what society assumes I am, and that is the answer they are looking for.

Many difficult situations have occurred throughout my lifetime because of what race people consider me to be, and the racism that I have faced because of it. However, it is almost an even bigger challenge for me to decide what I am for myself. I cannot even correctly say that I am half white and half Hispanic, because some days I feel more a part of one race than the other. Discovering and determining my identity continues to be a challenge, and will be for the rest of my life.

OVERCOMING HOMOPHOBIA

Anonymous

I first noticed my attraction to women at a young age. I distinctly remember sitting in front of the old TV with its carved wooden legs, wrapped up in my blanket, watching a commercial for Special K cereal. It was a tropical beach scene featuring a slender woman in a white bathing suit laying on a hammock. Suddenly, it occurred to me that I found the woman's body appealing. I thought this was strange; at that age I didn't know what homosexuality was. But having the attention span of a young child, I didn't dwell on the matter and soon forgot about it.

Until seventh grade, when I had my first crush on a girl. Sarah . . . she had the longest wavy red hair I had ever seen and a smile like sunshine and daisies. She was a year ahead of me in school, and she belonged to the crowd I desperately wanted to join. I'd watch for her in the lunchroom, hanging out in places where she might be. I thought of her constantly. Yet, I didn't think I was a lesbian. For one thing, I still liked guys. Secondly, I had read in those teen self-help "What's Happening to My Body" books that many kids experience same-sex crushes during puberty. Surely this was just a phase.

But in eighth grade, when my attraction to girls only grew stronger, I began to wonder. I sort of lost my sense of reality. In the present, I considered myself a lesbian; but when I looked to the future I could see nothing other than a well-adjusted, heterosexual adult having a good laugh over her little bout with lesbianism as a kid. I wavered continually between homo and hetero; it was always on my mind. It was distracting, vexing—I wished I could just forget about the whole thing. The possibility of bisexuality occurred to me, but I quickly pushed it aside. That would be worse than being a lesbian. In theory, I had no problem with homosexuals—but jeez, I didn't want to be one! See, I had this self-righteous attitude, thinking I was so liberal in my views on gays; but homophobia had been instilled in me just as it had in everyone else. The thought of being gay disgusted me.

In the struggle with my sexual identity I felt completely alone. It seemed there was no one who'd understand what I was going through that I could talk to. One day at school, I was with some friends in the hallway between classes. One girl was telling us how she had discovered her neighbor was bisexual. As I stood listening to everyone giggle and screech over the gory details, it really hit me what would happen if people knew about me. I never thought I could feel so alone with people all around me. Leaving the chattering cluster of girls, I went to a dark corner where I could cry. I'm someone who isn't good at dealing with and expressing emotions: I don't always cry when I need to. But that day, once I started, I couldn't stop. My crying fit lasted well into fourth hour. Afterwards, it felt like I had finally let out something that had been building up inside me for a long time. I felt exhausted, but good.

Throughout my eighth-grade year, I kept hoping it was just a phase. But there was no denying that I felt an attraction to both boys and girls; and gradually, I came to accept my bisexuality.

Now, a year later, I can even say I'm proud to be queer (I like the term "queer" because it includes everyone who isn't heterosexual). I've always thought of myself as a very open-minded person—someone who never shuts out a possibility or perspective. I think my bisexuality is one way in which this quality manifests itself. In fact, given the choice, I would not change. That is one thing I want to make clear: No one knows exactly what causes homosexuality or bisexuality, and it is in no way a conscious choice. Our sexual preference is something we have no control over, much like our ethnicity and gender. Therefore, prejudice against queers is as cruel and unjustified as racism and sexism.

So far, I've only told a few close friends. I'm waiting 'til I'm older to come out, because I want to be mature enough to handle the pain that will inevitably follow. I think my parents will be fairly understanding, but other relatives may virtually disown me. I will lose friends. As an adult, my job opportunities will be limited. If I have children, they might be taken away from me; or if I try to adopt I may be unable to do so. I will be harassed, maybe even assaulted. But I will be strong. I overcame my own homophobia; I will overcome that of others. I'll be true to myself, I won't stay silent, and I will not back down.

GUNS

for the country's
ixed. While there
vices to assist street
en table, her sitting,
ock, the interrogation began
me control over his future
~~tical~~ ~~behavior~~ ~~set in a~~
~~ptured~~
~~their arms~~ I
~~newspaper so much~~ here in
when he hit me. I'd
~~doctor and he~~ ~~kitchen table~~
lying in the hammock, the

GUNS

Both Kelly Hardy and Jake Reyo have had first hand experience of the destruction and injury that guns can cause. Kelly's brother shot himself, and Jake Reyo was shot when he walked out of his house to have a cigarette.

Kelly has learned from her experience what a "single bullet can do." Jake tells us that being shot brought him a new relationship with his father and a new school.

These stories are at the end of this book as a warning: We must find ways to make certain our kids do not have to live with the daily reality of gunfire. It is the least we can do for young people in this country to provide them with places of safety.

LIFE AS WE KNOW IT

Kelly Hardy

You will never think that a life-and-death situation can happen to you. Only when it reaches out and shocks you, daring you to meet the crisis. Believe me, when such a crisis occurs, it will hit you with full force. On July 6, 1991, my brother shot himself in the head with a .38 caliber gun.

It was a shining sunny day when I was helping my brother move from a crime filled area to a nice house in a residential area. I thought maybe the move would change him, rid him of his childhood antics. As we left the house, I would have never guessed that would be the first and last time in that house for my brother.

It was around 11:30 that night when we received a knock at the door. We were surprised to see a police officer standing on our doorstep. He just told us that Mike had an accident and to call Ramsey. My mother got on the phone right away. The nurse on the phone told us that Mike had been shot in the head and basically had no chance. With that statement in mind we jumped into the car and sped to the hospital. As soon as we got there Mike was being wheeled off to surgery. We started making phone calls to relatives and friends to let them know. I'm a very impatient person, so just sitting there in a little waiting room wasn't doing me any good. So I went in search of a pop machine. When I came back from there I noticed all these people sitting in the large waiting room. There were about thirty girls and eight guys. Then I realized that these were all of Mike's friends. I said hello to several of them and then went back into the family waiting room. A few hours later we received word that Michael was out of surgery. The doctor said that the situation would be touch-and-go for awhile. They had no idea of any complications that might bother him in the future. Luckily, there was none.

The next months were a total battle. Can you imagine having to learn to read, write, and walk again? Good for Mike, he still knew all those things—just needed a brush-up. Mike had to go rehabilitation for awhile there. Those nurses there loved and hated him. Loved him because he could sweet-talk anyone; hated him because he wouldn't take his medicine, ate the forbidden junk food, and would play his radio nonstop.

Mike is lucky to be alive. He received a second chance, a chance that many people don't get. Today, he still has half of a .38 caliber bullet in the back of his brain. He also has no skull on the left side of his head. I bet you are probably all wondering why he would do such a stupid thing. He and his friends were playing a game—Russian Roulette. Yes, that's right. I have no idea why people want to ruin their lives. I am not trying to tell you what to do. Just telling you the truth, the cold hard truth: Guns can kill. I hope my story etches the real reality of guns into your mind—just what a single bullet can do. It's a pure tragedy that so many young lives are wasted. Thrown away on someone else's stupidity for having and firing a gun.

During the months of wondering what the future would hold, there were two things that got us through it. The first was that we relied on the doctors and believed that they were always right. The second thing was one of the most important things of all—hope. Hope is something that everyone experiences or needs to experience when they go through life. It is an essential feeling that can take you through a difficult situation with the belief that you are going to get through that situation. And it was that feeling of hope that stayed with me.

MY CHALLENGE

Jake Reyo

I'll never forget it. It was Friday, and I was just chilling at my friend Jeff's house. We were playing Super Nintendo and I had paused the game to go outside and have a smoke. I was standing in the back yard because I could not smoke in the house and I was just about done when I heard this really loud noise like a firecracker. I had no clue as to what it was and then I blacked out.

I woke up at his kitchen table remembering nothing, not knowing what was going on. I was laying on the floor, and my stomach ached. Jeff hung up the phone and said, "All right, Jake, get up, they are here."

I said, "Who is here?"

"The police, the ambulance, and everybody."

I asked, "What for?"

Jeff said, "Jake you have been shot."

As I looked down at my chest there were so many different thoughts racing through my mind. Was all that pain coming from that little bitty hole? I didn't know if I should cry or just faint again.

As I walked to the front yard of Jeff's house I became really scared of death. Because I didn't want to die this young. I wouldn't have gotten to do all of the things that I wanted to do. Now, every night before I go to sleep, I always wonder what it would be like if I didn't make it out of the hospital. If I hadn't gotten shot, what kind of situation would I be in right now?

The trip to the hospital was not pleasant because of all the construction. The ambulance had to back out of the street at Jeff's house, and there were huge holes in the ground—kind of like they were digging for gold. The ride to the hospital was like being in a demolition derby. I could see all the trees flying by through the back window like they were in a tornado. Before I went into surgery the nurse asked if she could put a catheter in. I said yes, for no apparent reason.

The hospital was a very dreary sight for the first few days. I think all the morphine had a little to do with that. The most excruciating pain was when they took X-rays of my back and chest. It seemed like they were going to break my back in half. The weirdest feeling was when they took the chest pump line out of my chest. My innards felt like they were just being sucked out of me. The funniest thing about that part was that I did not remember the chest pump line going into me in the first place. When my doctor took out the staples from my stomach I thought that it would hurt but I couldn't feel a thing. There were two other disgusting things about my visit to the hospital. One of them was when they pulled out the catheter because it seemed like I was going to the bathroom all the time. The other was the taste from the naso-gastric tube after they pulled that out.

I realize now that the worst thing about this whole situation was that I could have hurt so many people that I love and care for, especially one person in particular, who I know has always been there for me and always will be there for me. I think getting shot made me realize how much I have loved her, but I don't think that she ever really knew that. If I had another chance to be in a relationship with her, it wouldn't take me more than a half of a second to decide what I would want to do, knowing what I know now. I would have told her about my love a long time ago, but I am not a person who can tell people how I feel.

The strangest thing about this whole situation is that I had to get shot for my father to come see me for the first time in fourteen years. I think this was very cruel. The first thing that he said to me was, "I see you have changed." For a minute I didn't understand what he was saying. He probably meant that I had grown up. The last time he had seen me was when I was only two years old. Actually, he looked like an overgrown dog that could talk. My mom's cousin said that he looks like Charles Manson.

I think that there are two reasons why I am alive. One of them is that I haven't done everything that I wanted to do in my life yet. Some of those things are moving out on my own, finishing high school, getting my license, having my own car, and getting a full-time job. The other reason has to do with my real father. It took him fourteen years and it took me to get shot before he would come and visit me. On the third day of laying in the hospital, I received a card and a letter from my father. I don't remember what the card said, but I do remember what the letter said. It said that he was really sorry that he didn't come and visit me before, and from now on, he and I will keep in touch like a father and son should. Toward the end of the letter, he wrote a small paragraph about my brother. It said "If you didn't all ready know, Josh, your brother, is not my biological son. You should ask your mother about that."

So I did ask her and she said that we would talk when we get home.

As I arrived at home my mom explained to me what happened between all of us in the past. She started to tell me the whole story about the night that she got pregnant and I said, "Just forget about how and tell me about why." She told me that she got really drunk when she was at a party and that one thing led to another and she was pregnant with my brother Josh. Then she said that she and my father told everybody that Josh was their child.

There is another positive thing about me getting shot, besides seeing my father again, and that is I had to switch schools. Coming to a different school is helping me get enough credits to graduate on time.

When I first started at this school, I was hanging out with a guy named Mo, and he was real cool about every thing. He showed me around and made me feel like I was at my home school with all my friends. For awhile it seemed like we were inseparable. He got me a job working at the Mall of America, which was all right but it grew old after a while. We visited the movie theater almost every day and I noticed that one of my best friends from my old high school, North, worked there. He was just as cool as he was when we were back in school together. It seemed back then that he was the only one who helped me get through my freshman year, which wasn't that bad. He and I hung out for a while and it seems like we are brothers. He understands what I've gone through, and he cares for me as if I was his little brother.